To Bill
from Martin

The Gospel and the Twelve Steps

Martin M Davis

MARTIN M. DAVIS

RPI Publishing, Inc.

Published by
Recovery Publications, Inc.
1201 Knoxville Street
San Diego, CA 92110-3718
(619) 275-1350

Library of Congress Cataloging-in-Publication Data
Davis, Martin M., 1948–
The Gospel and the twelve steps : developing a closer relationship with Jesus / Martin M. Davis.
p. cm.
Includes bibliographical references.
ISBN 0-941405-31-1 (pbk)
1. Twelve-step programs—Religious aspects—Christianity.
2. Recovering addicts—Religious life. I. Title.
BV4596.T88D38 1993
248.8′6—dc20 93-15977
CIP

Printed in the United States of America
First edition 10 9 8 7 6 5 4 3 2 1

To my wife,
Sara Allison Westbrook Davis

Acknowledgments

Through the years of my recovery, certain people have deeply influenced me; therefore, they have contributed greatly to what is written in the following pages. Now it is my privilege to acknowledge and thank them for the immeasurable contribution they have made to my life.

Evan Hanson, my beloved friend and fellow servant of the King, has been a formative influence. I recall the hours we spent sitting in the grass in the middle of the golf course—talking about God. My friend Jim Yancey delivered the therapeutic intervention that helped me realize that I could write a book. My friend Ron Mumbower's faith in me—and patience with me—gave me the unique opportunity to grow both as a Christian and as a therapist. I am grateful for the hours spent on Wednesday mornings with Evan, Jim, and Ron, sitting at the Round Table, preparing one another for our individual quests in the service of the King.

Ken Gilburth, my friend and wise counselor, guided me through a turbulent year in my life and profoundly influenced me. My friend David Grantham not only inspired me to go to seminary but also touched me deeply when he suggested I get out of my boat and into God's boat.

I am eternally indebted to my dear friend Martha Turner Copeland who introduced me to the Twelve Steps.

I am grateful to the members of the Big Twelve group who helped me struggle through the early years of recovery— Harold, Bill, Pat M., Gary, Charles, and Pat V.

I also thank Ron Halvorson, Bob Manley, and the staff of Recovery Publications, Inc., for giving me the opportunity to serve the King with my writing.

Finally, and foremost, I acknowledge and thank my wife Sara, to whom this book is dedicated. She has walked beside me faithfully and without complaint as I have struggled to find my true path in life. No one has been of greater support to me, and I am blessed to be married to her.

Martin M. Davis
Brandon, Mississippi
April, 1993

*The Twelve Steps of Alcoholics Anonymous**

1. We admitted we were powerless over alcohol—that our lives had become unmanageable.
2. Came to believe that a Power greater than ourselves could restore us to sanity.
3. Made a decision to turn our will and our lives over to the care of God *as we understood Him.*
4. Made a searching and fearless moral inventory of ourselves.
5. Admitted to God, to ourselves, and to another human being the exact nature of our wrongs.
6. Were entirely ready to have God remove all these defects of character.
7. Humbly asked Him to remove our shortcomings.
8. Made a list of all persons we had harmed, and became willing to make amends to them all.
9. Made direct amends to such people wherever possible, except when to do so would injure them or others.
10. Continued to take personal inventory and when we were wrong promptly admitted it.

11. Sought through prayer and meditation to improve our conscious contact with God, *as we understood Him,* praying only for knowledge of His will for us and the power to carry that out.

12. Having had a spiritual awakening as the result of these steps, we tried to carry this message to alcoholics, and to practice these principles in all our affairs.

Table of Contents

Introduction

The Twelve Steps and the various organizations that have sprung from them have become an important social force in today's society. Originally conceived by Bill Wilson, a cofounder of Alcoholics Anonymous (AA), these steps provide the framework of a program of recovery as currently practiced by numerous Twelve-Step organizations.

The spiritual principles embodied in the Twelve Steps exert a powerful influence in the lives of a vast number of people in recovery from various chemical, behavioral, and relationship addictions. Numerous self-help groups have developed that use the Twelve Steps of Alcoholics Anonymous as their model. Included among these Twelve-Step groups are Narcotics Anonymous, Cocaine Anonymous, Overeaters Anonymous, Codependents Anonymous, Anorexia-Bulimia Anonymous, Overspenders Anonymous, Adult Children of Alcoholics, and, of course, Al-Anon, the original sister group of AA.

Because of the rapid growth of these organizations and their relative success in facilitating recovery from various chemical, behavioral, and relationship addictions, many people in Twelve-Step programs have escaped the psychological, emotional, and spiritual prison that is addiction. Because of the emphasis these programs place on spiritual principles, many recovering persons have found their way into the Christian Church. I am one person who was led to Jesus Christ via the Twelve Steps.

Newcomers to Twelve-Step programs are introduced early on to the concept of a higher power. Soon thereafter, the phrase "God as we understand Him" is included in the program of recovery. For those outside Twelve-Step circles, including many evangelical Christians, the concept of a higher power is a source of confusion and often is viewed with skepticism.

To be sure, the term higher power may have many meanings, depending on who uses the term. The same may be said of the term "God." When the Twelve Steps were developed more than fifty years ago, "God" was largely conceived, at least in the United States, in traditional Judeo-Christian terms. With the influx of eastern thought into our society, beginning in the 1960s and continuing today in various forms of new age thinking, the traditional Judeo-Christian concept of God has come under attack. The effects of that attack are being felt in the many groups practicing the Twelve Steps. No longer can one be reasonably certain that the terms "higher power" and "God" are synonymous with the Divine Creator revealed in the Holy Bible.

The spiritual principles encompassed in the Twelve Steps are ways of life—patterns of living that daily inform our thoughts, feelings and actions. For many, myself included, the Twelve Steps were the pathway that led first to "God" in general, then, finally, to Jesus Christ in particular. This should not be surprising, for the spiritual principles encompassed in the Twelve Steps are not only a way of life that daily informs our thoughts, feelings, and actions, but also are squarely founded in *biblical* teaching, as this book will demonstrate.

The growth of AA and other Twelve-Step groups has been phenomenal. From its beginnings in the 1930s, with only a handful of members, AA alone has grown to a current worldwide membership of 1.8 million.[1] Many other Twelve-Step organizations also have experienced rapid growth. It cannot be accidental that the rapid rise of Twelve-Step programs, especially in the United States, exactly parallels the decline of the Christian Church as a meaningful influence in the lives of American citizens. The decreasing importance of the Church as a spiritual, psychological, and emotional force in our society has created a vacuum in many people's lives, which is now being filled by the various Twelve-Step organizations.

The cultural Christianity so commonly practiced today is a tepid, insipid mixture that lacks the power to invigorate people, whether spiritually, psychologically, or emotionally. While people *thirst* for the "water of life," our churches increasingly lack the capacity to provide it. Many now satisfy their thirst in the meeting rooms of the various Twelve-Step organizations.

Inherent in Twelve-Step groups is a strong social bonding and camaraderie characteristic of people who share an important, common interest. Because of their common background of addiction, whether chemical, behavioral, or relational, members of Twelve-Step groups rapidly "identify" with one another and easily form a bond of fellowship. As people united against a common enemy (addiction), they form a strong social unit from which all members draw strength. The social cohesion of the group, combined with its underlying foundation of "spirituality," creates a powerful entity, which frequently becomes *the* major influence in members' lives. The spiritual principles of the group are practiced in "all their affairs." The Twelve-Step program literally becomes a way of life.

Unfortunately, such is not the case for too many members of the group known as the Church. Like the Twelve-Step group, the Church was originally a close-knit social organization built upon a foundation of spirituality with Jesus Christ as the chief cornerstone. Members of the first-century Church commonly met in small groups, usually in someone's house. Their fellowship and social bonding were so strong that they "were together and had everything in common" (Acts 2:44) for the benefit of the members of the group. In those early days of the Church, Christianity was the way of life for its adherents, not merely something practiced on Sundays.

Churches today often lack the social cohesion and camaraderie—not to mention spirituality—of their first-century counterparts. These attributes, so familiar to the first-century Christian, are today more likely to be experienced in the Friday night Twelve-Step meeting held in the church's basement.

One of the many strengths of the Twelve-Step group is the acceptance experienced by its members. These are people all too familiar with the "pain, brokenness, and human limitation"[2] of life in modern society. They have walked a common path that has led them, and often their loved ones, through the wilderness of sorrow, grief, and pain. Because of the commonality of their past mistakes and all-too-human failings, participants of Twelve-Step programs are able to accept one another without judgment. Members are thus freed to be themselves, to be *real* rather than pretentious. They attribute their salvation from addiction not to their own efforts, but rather to the grace of God. They view recovery as a gift, not something merited. They willingly share their "experience, strength, and hope"[3] with any who wish to join them on their journey in recovery.

The acceptance found in the Twelve-Step group is sadly lacking in many churches. Instead of acceptance and understanding, those Christians who have succumbed to human weaknesses and shortcomings often experience social pillorying in the form of judgment, criticism, and gossip. The guilty but repentant Christian is all too often the subject of scorn, whispering, and backbiting, rather than the recipient of acceptance, understanding, and forgiveness.

The openness and honesty characteristic of the Twelve-Step group is frequently dangerous in some churches. These churches are often among the last places one would dare to be real and genuine! It seems that the churchgoer is expected to wear a smiley-faced mask and answer every inquiry as to one's condition with a superficial "We're all just fine!" "Unacceptable" thoughts, such as the doubt that occasionally nags every believer, often go unexpressed for fear of criticism. A man's struggle with sexual lust or a woman's battle with addictive tranquilizers dare not be mentioned for fear of censure and condemnation. "Unacceptable" emotions such as anger, perhaps with God or a spouse, are held inside and stuffed for fear that their expression would result in alienation and judgment. In short, we are too often justifiably afraid to be ourselves, warts and all, in church because we fear the consequences. Rather than serving as hospitals for the sick, too many churches shoot their wounded.

The Church can learn much from today's Twelve-Step groups. Many Christians would do well to emulate the nonjudgmental attitude of acceptance practiced by most (not all, of course) members of Twelve-Step programs. The "attitude of gratitude" routinely encouraged in Twelve-Step meetings would certainly benefit those who are heirs to the kingdom of God and adopted children of the King of the Universe. The camaraderie and social cohesion, once part of the early Church, but now more typical of the Twelve-Step group, is a shining model for today's Christian community. The attempts by members of Twelve-Step programs to practice spiritual principles in all their affairs must be emulated by all those who would make Christianity truly a *way* of life.

The Christian Church, however, has much to offer those who follow the spiritual principles embodied in the Twelve Steps. The Church is the guardian of both the Word of God—the Holy Bible—and the sacraments. Knowledge of the Holy Scriptures, God's word in written form, and the Sacraments, the message of salvation enacted in ritualized form, can provide the recovering addict the basis for *true* spirituality. Most importantly, the Christian Church promotes knowledge and understanding of the only truly legitimate higher power; that Higher Power is Jesus Christ himself. In him, and only in him, can one hope to live, both now and forever, a life characterized by true spirituality.

An increasing number of Twelve-Step practitioners are entering the Church today. These people wish to go beyond the often vague and mysterious concept of a higher power to a personal relationship with Jesus Christ. The Church can provide a means for developing that relationship by helping the new Christian to "grow in the grace and knowledge of our Lord and Savior Jesus Christ" (2 Pet. 3:18).

Just as the Church can provide a vehicle for growth, the experience, strength, and hope that recovering addicts bring to the Church can not only change the characteristic of the church group but greatly benefit it as well. Those who enter the Church from a background in the Twelve Steps can act as bridges or links between two groups of people who have historically been at odds.

For far too long, many evangelical Christians have looked down their noses at those who have succumbed to various chemical, behavioral, or relationship addictions. Evangelicals have viewed such persons as weak willed and derelict. Likewise, many members of Twelve-Step groups have, and continue, to view Christians as phonies or sanctimonious hypocrites. Because of their bad experience with traditional religion, the early members of AA refused to include any language in their program of recovery that reminded them of traditional religious concepts.[4]

Christians in recovery, those persons who have both a personal relationship with Jesus Christ and practice the Twelve Steps as part of their recovery from various addictions, are in a unique position to bridge the gap between the evangelical and Twelve-Step communities. To the Church, they provide models of nonjudgmental love, acceptance, and spirituality as a way of life; to the Twelve-Step community, they bring a personal relationship to the only true Higher Power, Jesus Christ. This book is written to these Christians in recovery. Although the language used is that of the Twelve Steps of Alcoholics Anonymous, the principles of recovery explored here are applicable to *all* Twelve-Step programs.

While written primarily with Christians in recovery in mind, this book is not intended for them only. Instead, it is written to *all* Christians, especially to those new in the faith, for it is a presentation of the Gospel of Jesus Christ in evangelical terms.

Perhaps most importantly, this book is written for those who practice the Twelve Steps, but who are not Christians. Through this presentation of the Gospel of Jesus Christ written within the framework of the Twelve Steps, it is sincerely hoped that those Twelve-Step followers who have been resistant to the Christian faith will find the familiar language contained herein a palatable means of coming to a saving relationship with Jesus Christ.

The purpose of this book is to demonstrate that the program of recovery known as the Twelve Steps and "the Way" of living that is called Christianity are identical—not two distinct and separate paths through life nor two mutually exclusive approaches to spirituality. Recovery is a process. Like all people living in this fallen world, therefore, we are not healed; yet, we are being healed one day at a time as we continue to practice these principles of recovery in everything that we do. The way that is called Christianity and the way of the Twelve Steps is the framework within which we live our lives twenty-four hours a day, seven days a week.

It is my ardent hope that after reading this book, Christians in recovery will no longer compartmentalize their lives into two divisions: one part being "the program" (the Twelve Steps) and the other being the Church. Christianity and the Twelve Steps are not competing world views. So long as Jesus Christ is one's Higher Power, each may be understood in terms of the other.

This book is also a call to all churches to establish their own Christians in Recovery groups. These groups may use biblical principles within a Twelve-Step framework to facilitate the continued recovery from addiction and the Christian growth of their members. Perhaps this book can be used toward that end.

Finally, this book is a call to all Christians in recovery to share the Gospel of Jesus Christ with the Twelve-Step community. We may start by always identifying our Higher

Power as Jesus Christ. The Holy Spirit will open the doors for sharing the Gospel as he deems appropriate. We, as Christians in recovery, are blessed to have a personal relationship with the only legitimate Higher Power there is. Let us use our unique position to share this blessing with our fellow Twelve-Step members as the Holy Spirit leads.

CHAPTER I

The Journey Begins

STEP ONE: *We admitted we were powerless over alcohol—that our lives had become unmanageable.*

The first step is difficult for many people entering a program of recovery from addiction. To admit that we are "powerless" and that our lives have become "unmanageable" is a particularly distasteful chore for most of us.

The values of our culture make this step even more difficult. Ours is a society that extols the virtue of the rugged individual. Throughout our history we have sung the praises of the self-made person who boldly charges forth to carve civilization from the savage wilderness: The explorer and the frontiersman were followed by the railroad magnate, the cattle baron, the corporate mogul, the high financier, the golden-haired goddess of stage and screen, and the seven-figured sports star as the heroes and icons of American culture. Thus barely have we embarked on a journey of Twelve Steps when we stumble headlong on the distinctly un-American ideas of powerlessness and unmanageability. In a society that worships the hero and the strong, the first step is a medicine that is not easily swallowed.

In addition to our cultural aversion to powerlessness, the admission of powerlessness is made yet even more difficult by three erroneous assumptions embedded deep in human nature and present from birth. Pastor John Keller, a minister who has worked with alcoholics for more than thirty years, summarizes these false assumptions:

> 1) I am in control or ought to be in control of all that has to do with my life; 2) I am the center of the universe; 3) Everything and everyone ought to be spinning around me so I can have what I want and life will be the way I want it to be.[1]

There is within each of us, therefore, a selfish, egocentric human nature that demands that life meet its expectations. Keller writes, "It is a matter of wanting to do it my way, but more than that, it is wanting it to be my way."[2]

Dr. Harry Tiebout, a psychiatrist who worked with alcoholics in the early years of AA, noted that the egocentricity and sense of omnipotence derived from these false assumptions are embedded deep in the human psyche. Tiebout referred to this innate egocentricity and sense of omnipotence as "his majesty the baby,"[3] a term we will encounter frequently in this book. This infantile grandiosity does not pass away with maturity; rather, "his majesty the baby" continues his tyrannical reign into adulthood.

> There is that within us that tenaciously wants to remain on the throne of our lives, our sense of omnipotence and egocentricity. In our words, attitudes, feelings and behaviors we can hear the infant, "his majesty the baby," inside sometimes shouting, "I want it my way. I want what I want. I want to be in control of all that has to do with my life, and I will prove that I am."[4]

To admit powerlessness, as is called for in the first step, runs contrary to our egocentric, omnipotent human natures.

Few of us willingly surrender our desire to be in control of our lives, to be at the center of our personally constructed universes. His majesty the baby does not abdicate his throne readily. Frequently, a "sufficient degree of pain"[5] is required to expel this tyrannical king from his throne.

WHAT POWERLESSNESS IS

Powerlessness is the inability to exert effective control over people, places, events, and things. In chemical dependency, powerlessness is the inability to control the use of a substance that threatens to destroy our lives. In addictive behaviors, such as compulsive gambling, powerlessness is the inability to control the compulsive behavior. In relationship addictions, powerlessness is the inability to control one's thoughts, feelings, and behaviors regarding another person.

In a much broader sense, however, powerlessness is the inability to control numerous aspects of our personal, social, and physical environment. Like it or not, we cannot control the thoughts, feelings, and behaviors of other adults; we cannot control the economy; we cannot control political events; we cannot control the weather; we cannot even add a single hour to our life spans. The world simply does not spin according to the dictates of our desires. The admission of powerlessness, therefore, is the *recognition* that we are not the center of the universe; that life is not the way we want it to be; that, in fact, we are largely unable to control people, places, events, and things all around us. Finally, the admission of powerlessness is the recognition of our finiteness and the inherent limitation of the human condition.

Powerlessness has to do with control or, more accurately, the lack of it. The desire to exercise control is inherent in human nature. Mastering the environment to a developmentally appropriate degree is one of the early tasks of childhood. Yet, in some situations and conditions, mastery or control are either inappropriate or no longer possible. For example, it is inappropriate to attempt to force another adult, in either overt or subtle ways, to behave in a prescribed manner. The desire to control the behavior of a significant other is a definitive characteristic of codependency. One of the first lessons learned by those entering Al-Anon (one of the first Twelve-Step programs) is that one cannot control the behavior of another adult. For example, when a loved one loses control due to the use of addictive chemicals, a behavioral change that is a hallmark of addiction, significant others are powerless to control his or her aberrant behavior. To desire control is not bad; in fact, varying degrees of control are necessary in a fallen and dangerous world. The desire for control in inappropriate or impossible situations, however, indicates a problem.

A discussion of the powerlessness associated with addictions such as alcoholism and other chemical dependencies inevitably raises questions about the nature of these dysfunctions. Are they diseases or are they merely weaknesses of the flesh springing from a lack of willpower?

An increasing number of mental health professionals view alcoholism and other chemical dependencies as bona fide diseases. Contributing to the disease model of chemical dependency are numerous scientific studies that demonstrate a genetic link in these disorders. Children of alcoholic parents, for example, are far more likely to become alcoholics themselves than are children of nonalcoholic parents. Studies show that the cross-generational transmission of these disorders cannot be attributed solely to environmental factors. Clearly, a genetic component is involved.

However, there are also environmental and social factors that contribute to the abuse of alcohol and other drugs. Among these are a background of familial dysfunction, lack of self-esteem, peer pressure, experimentation (curiosity), cultural influence, parental drug abuse, and a lack of moral and spiritual values.[6] These factors do not cause addiction, but they may facilitate its occurrence.

The disease model of addiction, however, sticks in the craw of many evangelical Christians. For example, many well-intentioned Christians view alcoholism as sin. They believe that practicing alcoholics are simply weak willed and unwilling to change their aberrant behavior. Yet to attribute alcoholism and other addictions to moral weakness or a lack of willpower is to grossly oversimplify complex neurological, behavioral, and spiritual issues.

Those of us who have succumbed to addiction are, in fact, *powerless* to control our use of addictive substances. That is the meaning of Step One! In trying to control our addiction to chemicals, we are hopelessly trying to control that which is beyond *our* power to control. In the midst of active addiction, *we* are beyond control. Control was forfeited somewhere in the foggy past as we unswervingly (or should I say "swervingly") marched down the road of addiction. The first step's admission of powerlessness is the *recognition* of our *inability* to control that which has surpassed *our* power to control.

Not only in chemical dependency are we confronted with our hopeless attempts to control that which is out of control, but also in behavioral and relationship addictions. The compulsive overeater, the compulsive overspender, or the compulsive gambler are all confronted with their total inability to control an out-of-control behavior. Those addicted to relationships are confronted time and again with their inability to control the thoughts, feelings, and behaviors of significant others. We are *all* powerless over innumerable people, places, events, and things.

It is important to realize, however, that an admission of powerlessness is not an admission of failure. Rather, it is an acknowledgment of our limitations as finite human beings. We are finally admitting that we are not God, that many aspects of our environment are beyond *our* ability to control.

When, as addicts ready for recovery, we are finally able to admit, "I am an addict, everything about me is an addict, and I am powerless over my addiction," we are in a position much like that described by the Apostle Paul. He, too, was acutely aware of his powerlessness; he found himself unable to do the good things he wished to do. His human nature often compelled him to do the sinful things from which he so longed to be free. He wrote, "What a wretched man I am! Who will rescue me from this body of death?" (Rom. 7:24)

The phrase "body of death" has various meanings. Some view it as a reference to one of the most horrible and sinister forms of criminal punishment used by the Roman government of Paul's day. For those criminals guilty of the highest offenses such as murder, the victim's body—a dead, rotting corpse—was chained to the perpetrator's legs. Criminals would thus be forced to spend their remaining days literally dragging around the putrid, festering bodies of their victims before they, too, died—often from the corpse's disease and decay. Thus Paul laments, "Who will rescue me from this body of death?" The body of death the Apostle Paul refers to is his own sinful, human nature—the same egocentric, omnipotent nature that plagues us all.

At Step One, we addicts are in the same position as Paul; we are manacled to a dying, addicted lifestyle. The admission of powerlessness required by Step One is a recognition that the old, addictive lifestyle must die and that, if we are to live new lives of recovery, the chains that have bound us to the old way of life must be broken! With our admission of powerlessness comes the implicit acknowledgment that *we* cannot break the chains of addiction ourselves; only a power greater than ourselves can do that!

In his inspired wisdom, the Apostle Paul encapsulates the first *three* steps when he writes:

> What a wretched man I am! [Step One] Who will rescue me from this body of death? [Step Two] Thanks be to God—through Jesus Christ our Lord! [Step Three] (Rom. 7:24–25)

WHAT POWERLESSNESS IS NOT

It is essential, to both our recovery and our self-esteem, to understand that powerlessness is *not* a lack of willpower. Neither is it a lack of strength, nor a lack of determination. Powerlessness is not a lack of ability or talent. As we shall see in the following pages, even persons of extraordinary strength, ability, and talent have found themselves powerless over people, things, and events.

Many persons outside Twelve-Step programs, and even many just coming into these programs, think of powerlessness in terms of willpower or, more accurately, as a lack of willpower. Powerlessness and willpower, however, are totally unrelated concepts. Comparing these two ideas is like comparing apples and oranges; they are not the same. Willpower is tight-jawed, teeth-grinding determination. Powerlessness, to the contrary, is the inability to exert effective control, even when accompanied by our most tenacious efforts.

How many of us, ravaged by an addiction to alcohol, drugs, food, or compulsive behaviors, have white-knuckled our way past sleepless nights, weeks, and months, only to succumb once again to the power of an addiction? How often have we achieved prolonged periods of abstinence, perhaps even as much as a year, by doggedly exerting the force of our wills, only to find ourselves once again caught helplessly in the grip of an overpowering addiction? It takes tremendous willpower to sustain any prolonged period of abstinence when every cell in our body or every thought in our mind is screaming for a fix. Yet even in the face of these colossal efforts to maintain abstinence through the sheer power of will, we finally succumb once again to the overpowering demands of our addiction. As those of us who are addicted to substances and compulsive behaviors have demonstrated, hope for recovery springs to life only when we finally and knowingly admit our powerlessness.

Paul and Powerlessness

The Apostle Paul was a man of determined will and dedication. Prior to his conversion to Christianity, he persecuted scores of Christians on behalf of those Jewish leaders who wished to stamp out the budding new religion of Christianity. Paul, whose name at that time was Saul, was even present at the murder of Steven, the first Christian martyr. After his traumatic confrontation with the Lord Jesus on the road to Damascus, Paul became a Christian (*see* Acts 9:1–18). Then, with all the enthusiasm with which he had formerly persecuted the Church of God (*see* Gal. 1:13), he used his energy and zeal in the service of the Lord Jesus Christ.

A brief examination of the details of Paul's life reveals a man of iron *will,* as well as dauntless courage. During his various missionary journeys throughout Asia Minor and Greece, Paul withstood severe trials and hardships in spreading the Gospel of Jesus Christ. He was thrown in jail, flogged numerous times, beaten with sticks, shipwrecked, threatened by robbers and criminals, persecuted by his own countrymen as well as by foreigners, and often went without food and water—all as part of his mission as apostle to the Gentiles (*see* 2 Cor. 11:22–27). In the face of such courage and willpower, one of the last traits we would attribute to Paul is powerlessness! Remember, however, that powerlessness has *nothing* to do with strength or courage or will.

In Paul's letter to the church in Rome, we find a different description of the man who endured the hardships described above. The man of iron will and incredible courage—who, year after year, endured beatings, shipwrecks, hunger, and persecution—knew exactly what it meant to be *powerless.* Even Saint Paul, years after coming to Christ, still struggled with sin and human limitation. Even this great saint faced situations over which he was powerless and totally unable to exert effective control. Paul described it this way:

> We know that the law is spiritual; but I am unspiritual, sold as a slave to sin. I do not understand what I do. For what I want to do I do not do, but what I hate I do . . . For I have the desire to do what is good, but I cannot carry it out. For what I do is not the good I want to do; no, the evil I do not want to do—this I keep on doing. (Rom. 7:14–15, 18b–19)

Paul is saying that his sinful human nature holds him *powerless* to do the things he wants to do.

We should begin to understand now that powerlessness is in a different category from concepts such as willpower and strength. The life of the Apostle Paul demonstrates that one can possess iron will, courage, and incredible endurance and, at the same time, be powerless over people, places, events, and things. Our powerlessness, therefore, is not something to be hidden or to be ashamed of—it is an inherent part of the human condition. By admitting powerlessness, we are not admitting that we are less than others or that we are inferior in any way. We are simply and honestly admitting that we are not God, that there are things in this universe—many things—that are completely beyond *our* control. Addiction is among those things.

OUR RESPONSIBILITY

As stated earlier, the disease concept of chemical dependency and addiction has gained wide acceptance in the mental health field. Yet the disease concept has been abused by many an ill-intentioned addict to provide an excuse for aberrant behavior: "I have a disease; I can't help it." Fortunately, however, the disease concept of chemical dependency has undergone important refinements. On the subject of alcoholism, Dr. Sandra D. Wilson writes:

> The disease concept has been refined in recent years to correct the false impression that alcoholism can be treated in such a way that alcoholic individuals do not have anything to do for themselves. This refinement views alcoholism as a chronic illness wherein the alcoholic is not the passive recipient of a cure, but instead is an active participant who assumes major responsibility for managing his or her own illness.[7]

As surely as many of us were irresponsible under the influence of active addiction, so now are we completely responsible for actively pursuing our individual recoveries. Powerlessness is not an excuse for failing to take personal responsibility for the management of our illness. During the throes of active addiction, we were incapable of managing our own lives. Now that we are in recovery, however, we can each accept that personal responsibility by recognizing that, while we are powerless over addiction, we are not powerless over *recovery.* We can assume active responsibility for managing our illness by practicing the spiritual, biblical principles of the Twelve Steps.

NOT FAILURE

Finally, we must understand that powerlessness is not failure. It was our stubborn refusal to admit our powerlessness that kept us helpless at the hands of addiction. The humble, honest admission of powerlessness is the first step in snatching victory from the jaws of defeat. Failures throw up their hands and say, "It's no use; there's no hope. Nothing can help me." Those of us on the path of recovery throw up our hands as well and honestly admit that all our desperate attempts at abstinence have gotten us nowhere. Yet upon admitting our total defeat at the hands of addiction—and this is the crucial difference—we begin to look outside ourselves, to a Power greater than ourselves, and inside us is born the shining hope that there may be a way after all! Like the phoenix rising gloriously from the ashes, our eyes turn heavenward with a renewed hope that a Power greater than ourselves can restore us to sanity.

Descent into Powerlessness

STEP ONE: *We admitted we were powerless over alcohol—that our lives had become unmanageable.*

HOW GOD USES POWERLESSNESS

Though it may seem astonishing to think so, rock-bottom powerlessness is often the means by which God transforms us into vessels for his use. While the world, in arrogance, scorns defeat, those of us in recovery may look back one day to discover that hitting rock bottom was the event that enabled us to bounce forward toward a new life. The pain and despair of powerlessness may be the means by which God *convinces* us of our need for restoration and healing.

The descent into addiction is more devastating and longer lasting for some than for others. In any case, the fiery crucible that is powerlessness and defeat allows God to convert raw material into pure gold. The alchemists of old tried unsuccessfully for centuries to convert base metals into gold;

yet, God performs successful transformations daily as active chemical dependents and other addicts enter the refining fire of Step One. God can use powerlessness as the first step in the lifelong process of transformation that converts us into fit vessels for his use.

Events in the lives of two biblical personalities and a contemporary Christian will illustrate how God uses powerlessness to accomplish his will.

Joseph

We begin in the Book of Genesis with the story of Joseph, the youngest of the twelve sons born to the patriarch Jacob (also called Israel).

Born when Jacob was old, Joseph was his father's favorite son. It was especially for Joseph that Jacob made the famous "coat of many colours" (as the old King James version of the Bible describes it). Not only was Joseph the baby of the family, but he probably was spoiled by the doting, aged Jacob. Joseph's older brothers were jealous of the special favor he found with their father.

An intense sibling rivalry had developed by the time the seventeen-year-old Joseph had two dreams that were to be the beginning of many troubles for him. In the first dream, Joseph saw his older brothers, represented by sheaves of grain, bowing down to him (*see* Gen. 37:5–7), and he related this dream to his brothers. Imagine the reaction of the older brothers to the dream of this young upstart. Moreover, Joseph was probably arrogant and cocky in telling this dream to his jealous brothers. To make matters worse, Joseph had another dream that made him appear even more arrogant and cocksure. In the second dream, his parents as well as his brothers bowed down to him (*see* Gen. 37:9)! This time, the shiny-faced young Joseph told not only his brothers but also his father about his latest dream. The dreaming boy was soundly rebuked by his father for a dream that must have inflated the teenager's already large ego.

Sometime thereafter, the older brothers were herding sheep near a neighboring village when, in the distance, they saw their upstart younger brother coming toward them. Years of anger, jealousy, and resentment must have boiled to the surface as they conceived a plan to murder their arrogant, dreaming brother. Reuben, the eldest of Jacob's sons, interceded and cautioned his brothers against shedding Joseph's blood. The others heeded the counsel of their older brother and agreed not to kill Joseph; instead, they seized Joseph and threw him into a dry well (*see* Gen. 37:12–24). This incident marked the beginning of the starry-eyed Joseph's descent into sorrow and powerlessness.

The image of Joseph lying helpless at the bottom of the well is a perfect example of powerlessness—Joseph had both literally and figuratively hit rock bottom. His arrogance and cocksuredness slowly began to melt away as he peered up out of the darkness of the pit toward the light above. Yet this frightening experience was only the beginning of Joseph's sorrows. His acquaintance with powerlessness had only just begun.

Soon after throwing Joseph into the well, the older brothers saw a caravan of spice traders approaching. They retrieved Joseph from the well and sold him to the traders for a mere eight ounces of silver (*see* Gen. 37:25–28). Now Joseph was a slave, the property of traders bound for Egypt. He was probably placed in chains to prevent his escape as the caravan plodded slowly to the great land of the Nile. Joseph had endless hours to reflect on his hopeless condition as the caravan made the weeks-long journey through the desert.

The chains and manacles that ground into his skin instilled both humility and pain as Joseph's descent into powerlessness deepened.

Upon arriving in Egypt, Joseph was sold to Potiphar, a captain of Pharoah's guard. For a while things fared better for Joseph. He achieved a position of responsibility and relative comfort in the home of his Egyptian master. His journey into darkness, however, was not over yet.

Potiphar's wife was attracted to the handsome, young Joseph and made sexual advances toward him. To his credit, Joseph refused to "do such a wicked thing" as to sleep with his master's wife (*see* Gen. 39:9–10). After continued rejection, Potiphar's wife falsely accused Joseph of making sexual advances toward her, the very thing she had done unsuccessfully to Joseph! Potiphar believed his wife's story and, in a fit of anger, had Joseph thrown into prison. Once again, Joseph found himself in a state of abject powerlessness.

Joseph's situation was one of increasing despair. Once in the pampered position of favorite son, he had since been forced into slavery and, finally, prison. To Joseph, God must have seemed far, far away.

The brevity of the biblical account may cause us to overlook the horror that Joseph experienced in prison: the squalid, filthy living conditions; the distasteful food; the disgusting smell; the rats. Two full years in those horrid conditions must have seemed like an eternity to the young man.

One day, Pharaoh, the king of the Egyptian empire, had an ominous dream that troubled him greatly. His cupbearer—who had been in prison with Joseph and, at that time, had had a dream that Joseph accurately interpreted—told Pharaoh about Joseph's ability to interpret dreams. Anxious to understand the meaning of his dream, Pharaoh sent for

Joseph. With God's help, Joseph was able to interpret the king's dream (*see* Gen. 41:15–16).

Pharaoh recognized that God was with Joseph and that "there [was] no one so discerning and wise" as Joseph (*see* Gen. 41:39). Pharaoh placed him in charge of his palace and all the people of Egypt. Joseph had become prime minister of the greatest empire on earth (*see* Gen. 41:41–43). He remained in that position until he died.

How could the helpless boy lying dusty and dirty at the bottom of the well imagine where his destiny would lead him? How could Joseph, bound in the chains of slavery, foresee what God had in store for him? How could the prisoner in Pharaoh's dark, damp dungeon have hoped ever to see the light of day, much less imagine himself as prime minister of Egypt?

Joseph's acquaintance with powerlessness was a long one. He was near the age of seventeen when he was thrown into the well, yet he "was thirty years old when he entered the service of Pharaoh king of Egypt" (Gen. 41:46). For well over ten years, Joseph learned the meaning of powerlessness. During that time, his arrogance and cocksuredness—character defects that contributed to his problems—evaporated in the crucible of slavery and imprisonment. The descent into the pit of powerlessness transformed the naive, shiny-faced boy into the mature, wisened, and humbled man who took leadership of Egypt under Pharaoh.

Many years later, Joseph's youthful dreams came true when his brothers came to Egypt looking for food in a time of famine. They bowed down before the powerful prime minister of Egypt, not recognizing their own flesh and blood (*see* Gen. 42:1–9). Rather than taking revenge for what had been done to him, however, Joseph demonstrated great nobility of character by forgiving his brothers and providing them food and material goods to see them through the famine (*see* Gen. 50:15–21).

In his position as prime minister, Joseph was able to avert the terrible tragedy that threatened Egypt and neighboring lands because of the famine. Because of Joseph's wise planning, many lives were saved, including the lives of his father and brothers.

In one of the more profound verses in the Old Testament, Joseph, looking back over his life and all that had happened to him, said to the brothers that had sold him into slavery, "You intended to harm me, but *God* intended it for *good* to accomplish what is now being done, the saving of many lives" (Gen. 50:20, emphasis added).

The story of Joseph teaches those of us in recovery that powerlessness is a tool used by God to work his will in our lives. The descent into powerlessness, the slavery of chemical dependency, and the prison of addiction may all be used by God to transform our lives so that we can become the persons he has always intended us to be. Arrogance, egotism, grandiosity, and the other character defects associated with active addiction melt away as we recognize and admit our powerlessness. As with Joseph, God often takes us to the bottom of the well so that he can accomplish *good* in our lives.

> And we know that in all things God works for the good of those who love him, who have been called according to his purpose. (Rom. 8:28)

Another Look at Paul

The above verse was penned by the Apostle Paul, under the inspiration of the Holy Spirit. We have already been introduced to this man of iron will, strength, and dedication.

In order to further our understanding of how God *uses* powerlessness, let's now take a detailed look at Paul's dramatic conversion on the road to Damascus.

Paul—or Saul, as he was called prior to his conversion—was a leading member of the Jewish group known as the Pharisees. He was a highly educated man who had studied under the great Jewish teacher, Gamaliel. Saul was empowered by the Sanhedrin (a Jewish legislative body) to actively seek out members of the new, rival religion of Christianity and imprison them. Saul was greatly feared by Christians because of the zeal with which he persecuted them.

The Book of Acts, chapter 9, describes Saul's dramatic conversion to Christianity and his experience of utter powerlessness. Saul was on his way to Damascus hoping to locate and imprison Christians.

> As he neared Damascus on his journey, suddenly a light from heaven flashed around him. He fell to the ground and heard a voice say to him, "Saul, Saul, why do you persecute me?"
>
> "Who are you, Lord?" Saul asked.
>
> "I am Jesus, whom you are persecuting," he replied. "Now get up and go into the city, and you will be told what you must do."
>
> . . . Saul got up from the ground, but when he opened his eyes he could see nothing. So they led him by the hand into Damascus. For three days he was blind, and did not eat or drink anything. (Acts 9:3–9)

Saul—the renowned scholar, the student of Gamaliel, the dreaded persecutor of Christians—had to be led by the hand, like a helpless child, to Damascus. Blind and so traumatized that he could neither eat nor sleep, Saul intimately experienced powerlessness.

A Christian named Ananias was used by God to restore Saul's vision and nourish him back to health.

Saul's traumatic conversion on the road to Damascus clearly exemplifies how God turns greatness into meekness, pride into humility, and strength into powerlessness. Saul's blind descent into the dark abyss of powerlessness was the means by which he was turned to the true Higher Power.

It is when we hit bottom that our thoughts turn upward; it is when we become blind that we are able to see! When, like Saul, we lay helpless in the dust of the road, we are finally able to swallow our pride. Then we may transcend the bounds of egocentricity so that a Power greater than ourselves can restore us to sanity!

Sometime later, the Lord told Paul:

> My grace is sufficient for you, for my power is made perfect in weakness. (2 Cor. 12:9)

A Contemporary Christian

As we have seen thus far, the descent into the abyss of powerlessness was the means by which God radically changed the lives of both Joseph and Paul. In the dark abyss, these men were transformed to prepare them to meet their destinies. A contemporary example may help fully drive home the point that God uses powerlessness for his purposes.

Charles Colson is founder and president of Prison Fellowship. This Christian ministry brings the Gospel of Jesus Christ to those in prison and seeks to improve conditions in prisons throughout the world. Colson is the author of numerous books, including *Born Again, Loving God,* and *Kingdoms in Conflict.* In his books, Colson has written extensively about his imprisonment, which was indirectly associated with the Watergate scandal of the early 1970s.

As a high-ranking official in the Nixon administration, Colson had served as a special counsel to the president. He held a position of power and prestige. His office was in the

White House itself, and the president of the United States called him by his first name. Colson had risen to the top; the American dream had come true for him. But then came the fateful Watergate scandal, which led to the collapse of the Nixon administration. Colson and others were sentenced to prison.

Charles Colson's descent into powerlessness was a deep one—from a powerful office in the White House to a prison cell. In this state of powerlessness, Colson came to know a Power greater than himself; while in prison, Charles Colson came to know the Lord Jesus Christ.

Colson has commented in his writings about the ironic twist his life has taken. He wrote about the thoughts he had one day in particular as he awaited his turn to speak at a prison chapel service:

> As I sat on the platform, waiting my turn at the pulpit, my mind began to drift back in time . . . to scholarships and honors earned, cases argued and won, great decisions made from lofty government offices. My life had been the perfect success story, the great American dream fulfilled. But all at once I realized that it was *not* my success God had used to enable me to help those in this prison, or in hundreds of others just like it. My life of success was not what made this morning so glorious—all my achievements meant nothing in God's economy. No, the real legacy of my life was my biggest failure—that I was an ex-convict. My greatest humiliation—being sent to prison—was the beginning of God's greatest use of my life. He chose the one experience in which I could not glory for his glory.
>
> Confronted with this staggering truth, I discovered in those few moments in the prison chapel that my world was turned upside down. I understood with a jolt that I had been looking at life backward. But now I could see: only when I lost everything I thought made Chuck Colson a great guy

> had I found the true self God intended me to be and the true purpose of my life.[1]

In prison, in defeat and humiliation, in total powerlessness, Charles Colson's life was transformed. Since that time, through both Prison Fellowship and his numerous books, Colson has helped spread the gospel of Jesus Christ throughout the world. Also, as a ministry to both soul and body, Prison Fellowship has brought about improvements in the living conditions of those in prison. Charles Colson is a contemporary example of how God uses the crucible of powerlessness for his life-transforming purposes. In the words of Jesus himself:

> Whoever finds his life will lose it, and whoever loses his life for my sake will find it. (Matt. 10:39)

As stated previously, powerlessness is the inability to exert effective control over people, places, events, and things. Said another way, powerlessness is Joseph in the well; it is Saul, helpless and blind in the dust of the Damascus road; it is Charles Colson in a prison cell. Most importantly, it is the means by which God changes lives, the means by which destiny is rerouted, and the first step in our program of recovery.

Powerlessness is not something to be denied, ashamed of, or regretted; it is something to be *admitted.*

. . . . CHAPTER III

A Hole in the Soul

STEP ONE: *We admitted we were powerless over alcohol—that our lives had become unmanageable.*

UNMANAGEABILITY

The first step also says "we admitted . . . that our lives had become unmanageable." The idea of unmanageability conjures up images of broken promises, failed commitments, destroyed relationships, unpaid bills, legal troubles, and wrecked physical health. Unmanageability includes all these consequences and many more that pertain to the personal, social, and material areas of life.

As I envision someone whose life has become unmanageable, I see a man running in blinding rain and dark, howling wind, lightning striking all around. As he rushes into his small cabin and slams shut the door against the storm, the wind blows his windows out. Chemical dependents and other addicts know what that storm feels like.

The idea of unmanageability, however, goes beyond the personal, social, and material spheres to include a kind of unmanageability that can destroy the soul. This kind of unmanageability brings with it a *spiritual* emptiness that results from the prolonged, self-centered lifestyle that plagues addicted people. Thus unmanageability includes an impoverishment of the spirit, a bankruptcy of the *soul*! Addiction—whether chemical, behavioral, or relational—impairs more than mental, emotional, or physical functioning. For those whose lives have become unmanageable, addiction leaves a spiritual emptiness, a gnawing *hollowness* inside. To borrow the words of T.S. Eliot, addicts are "the hollow men." Their lives are bereft of meaning and purpose, leaving their souls empty and hungry. Too often, their recourse has been to medicate the pain of soul-emptiness by engaging in further addictive behavior.

Unmanageability is not often thought of as soul-emptiness or life bereft of meaning. Yet the meaninglessness of life that commonly accompanies addiction is of far more serious consequence than unpaid drunken-driving tickets or unanswered demands for back child-support payments. Unmanageability goes beyond the immediate and apparent into the realm of the transcendent. Addiction has cost us far more than broken relationships or loss of material goods. Addiction is a prison of the soul. It separates that which is eternal within us from the Higher Power that is the wellspring of life. Ideas about unmanageability must include the *spiritual* as well as the mental, emotional, and physical arenas of life.

The Richest Man in the World

To illustrate that unmanageability involves much, much more than the apparent chaos in the personal, social, and material realms, let us consider a man whose life might seem anything but unmanageable—the richest, wisest man in the ancient world, Solomon, king of Israel.

The Book of Ecclesiastes, found in the Old Testament and written by King Solomon, is a remarkable illustration of the emptiness of life lived strictly on the horizontal plane, that is, in the material/physical realm only. We must remember that this book was written by one whose wealth and wisdom were legendary, even in his own lifetime. The glory and opulence of Solomon's riches, as well as the wisdom of his royal proclamations, were famous throughout the known world. Solomon had it all. The gold, silver, jewels, and other material possessions of this king were indescribable. "King Solomon was greater in riches and wisdom than all the other kings of the earth" (1 Kings 10:23). As if all this weren't enough, Solomon also had 700 wives and 300 mistresses! Before going further, I encourage you to read 1 Kings, chapter 10, to get the full impact of Solomon's riches. A grasp of the vast wealth and the material and sensual pleasures experienced daily by this man is essential to an appreciation of the bitter irony in his following words:

> "Meaningless! Meaningless!" says the Teacher [Solomon]. "Utterly meaningless! Everything is meaningless." (Eccles. 1:2)

How could a man who "had it all" write such words of soul-hollow despair?

> I, the Teacher, was king over Israel in Jerusalem. I devoted myself to study and to explore by wisdom all that is done under heaven . . . I have seen all the things that are done under the sun; all of them are meaningless, a chasing after the wind. (Eccles. 1:12–14)

Many addicts will understand what it means to "chase after the wind," to look for meaning on the horizontal plane of life. Solomon had the financial means to do or have whatever his heart desired. He not only had it all, he had tried it all: wine, women, laughter and folly, the amassing of all kinds of possessions, the undertaking of great public works (*see* Eccles. 2:1–9)—everything he could imagine to fill the emptiness of his soul. Solomon denied himself nothing; he refused his heart no pleasure. Yet with all that, he found life meaningless, a chasing after the wind (*see* Eccles. 2:10–11).

The entire book of Ecclesiastes reeks of the hopelessness, the despair, the utter emptiness of soul that plagued King Solomon as his life became increasingly futile, meaningless, and unmanageable. Clearly, though he possessed great worldly power and riches, Solomon was a man who ultimately lived to experience the rock bottom of powerlessness and unmanageability. Solomon's encounter with powerlessness and unmanageability was not the result of the loss of his family, his friends, his job, or his reputation. He had not been sentenced to jail or compelled to perform menial public service tasks as an act of restitution. His health and mental faculties remained stable. His desperate words make it clear, however, that his life had become unmanageable—soul-empty and bereft of meaning.

As we draw near the end of our discussion of the first step and prepare to consider the Higher Power of the second step, it is appropriate to explore why Solomon was in the existential dilemma of abject meaninglessness:

> As Solomon grew old, his [pagan] wives turned his heart after other gods, and his heart was not fully devoted to the Lord his God, as the heart of David his father had been. (1 Kings 11:4)

Solomon had turned from the source of meaning; he had forsaken the wellspring of life; he had severed his vertical connection and vainly sought meaning in the material and sensual realms.

Therefore, as Solomon's soul-hollow words ring in our ears, our conception of unmanageability must broaden. Admitting that our lives have become unmanageable is acknowledging the personal, social, material, and spiritual decay that is part and parcel of addiction.

The admission of powerlessness and unmanageability is neither a sign of weakness nor a source of shame; it is a recognition of reality—a *conviction of need* for healing and restoration. Christians in recovery, and others participating in Twelve-Step programs, must confront a reality of the human condition: that life is precarious and frail and, alone, each of us is able to manage very little.

> The race is not to the swift or the battle to the strong, nor does food come to the wise or wealth to the brilliant or favor to the learned; but time and chance happen to them all. (Eccles. 9:11)

CHAPTER IV

Only One Way

STEP ONE: *We admitted we were powerless over alcohol—that our lives had become unmanageable.*

We have seen that Solomon's existential dilemma, the hollowness of his soul, was closely connected to his horizontal view of life. He had lost his vertical connection. "His heart was not fully devoted to the Lord his God" (1 Kings 11:4).

When we addicts experience powerlessness and unmanageability, we are in much the same predicament as was Solomon—life is devoid of meaning. As addicts, we often sought meaning through use of chemicals or by engaging in compulsive behaviors. When we hit bottom, the emptiness of soul becomes acutely and painfully apparent. Bottomed out and powerless, our lives depend on finding a remedy for the gnawing emptiness inside us. If our compulsive behavior is to cease, it is essential that something fill the void inside us so that recovery may be possible. Like Joseph peering up from the depths of the well, when we hit bottom, we must look up toward "a Power greater than ourselves" if we are to be restored to sanity. Only a higher power can provide true meaning in life and solve our existential dilemma.

By its very nature, the soul seeks its home in the presence of the Transcendental Power that can restore it to sanity. In recovery, our spirits break free and soar over the walls of the prison that is addiction, thirsty for a relationship with the higher power. "As the deer pants for streams of water," writes the psalmist, "so my soul pants for you, O God" (Ps. 42:1).

Yet what is the nature of this higher power that we so desperately hope can restore us to sanity? In what or in whom did the pioneers of the Twelve Steps come to believe as they sought relief from the misery of their addictions? Who or what, after all, is this mysterious higher power?

HIGHER POWER?

The amorphous, vague higher power spoken of in Twelve-Step circles is often offensive to evangelical Christians—and not without justification. In many instances, the concept of a higher power has been trivialized and far removed from the position of respect in which it was held in the pioneering days of the Twelve Steps.

In 1935, when Alcoholics Anonymous was founded, America was under the strong influence of a traditional Judeo-Christian concept of God. We proclaimed ourselves to be "one nation under God" and routinely sought his blessing in both public and private affairs. Since the 1960s, however, our esteem and respect for God has greatly eroded. Part of that diminishment of reverence is seen in the all-too-frequent trivialization of the higher power of the Twelve Steps. In one Twelve-Step meeting, for example, I heard a man say that his "higher power" was his shiny, new pickup truck! I have even heard another person claim his swimming pool as his higher power! Apparently, some forget that chemical dependency and many other addictions are progressive and fatal diseases. Recovery is not amenable to the trivialization of an absolutely *essential* component of the Twelve-Step program. While swimming pools and pickup trucks may provide pleasant, temporary diversions, they will not restore one to sanity. It takes *power* to facilitate recovery, and that power must be *greater than* ourselves. Those who reduce the higher power to a lifeless, inanimate object are playing a dangerous game that makes them little different from primitive people worshiping wood or stone.

Not much better is some people's tendency to refer to the higher power as "H.P." or "Hal." This tendency to reduce the higher power to some sort of cosmic good buddy is little better than the pickup truck approach to the higher power described above. I firmly believe that a power that can restore us to sanity, that can fill the gnawing void inside us, is worthy of more than a modicum of respect.

Twelve-Step programs like that of AA make much of the fact that they involve "spiritual" principles. Addiction, after all, is a disease of the soul or spirit as well as the mind and body. It is when we enter the realm of the spirit that the higher power must be approached in realistic and reverent terms. In whose terms, however, are we to consider the higher power that can restore us to sanity?

In the arena of religion, our society is increasingly pluralistic. The God in whom we trust wears an increasingly diversified array of costumes. The Judeo-Christian concept of God, held by most (if not all) of our founding fathers, is faced with an onslaught of competing concepts that view God far differently from traditional Protestant or Catholic perceptions. As a result of the growing number of immigrants from far-eastern and near-eastern cultures, Twelve-Step meetings in large metropolitan cities like New York, Los Angeles, or Atlanta may be composed of Muslims, Hindus, Buddhists, and Christians. These persons are likely to hold very different views about God or the higher power. (Meetings may even include an occasional "new ager" who thinks he is the higher power!) What are Christians in recovery to do when faced with such an array of higher powers, with so many "gods" seeking worship and reverence?

As a Christian in recovery myself, I do not hesitate to state that my Higher Power is not a vague, amorphous, or mysterious concept. He is, in fact, the "image of the invisible God" (Col. 1:15). He is the divine Word or *Logos* who "became flesh and made his dwelling among us" (John 1:14). He is the one and only Son of God (*see* John 3:16). He has a name—and that name is not "Hal" or "H.P." His name is Jesus Christ! Furthermore, I believe that "salvation is found in no one else, for there is no other name under heaven given to men by which we must be saved" (Acts 4:12). Peter spoke these words in reference to Jesus Christ of Nazareth. I believe that not only is there salvation in no one else, but also that Jesus Christ is the only legitimate Higher Power that can restore us to sanity.

Now, speaking to my recovering brothers and sisters in Christ, this is not an invitation to take your Bible to the next Twelve-Step meeting and whack a Muslim or a Buddhist over the head with it! Our approach to the many higher powers that we may encounter in Twelve-Step meetings should closely resemble the diplomatic, peace-seeking approach used by the Apostle Paul.

On his second "missionary journey," one of the many cities the Apostle Paul visited was Athens, the capital of Greece. By the first century A.D., Greek or Hellenistic culture had spread throughout most of the known world. The pantheon of gods reverenced by the Greeks (Zeus, Poseidon, Aphrodite, Hermes, and so forth) stood in stark contrast to the one God of Judaism and Christianity. It is probable that a highly educated and traveled man like Paul was familiar with the polytheistic religion of Athens as he sought to spread the gospel of Jesus Christ to the epicenter of Greek culture.

The story of Paul's visit to Athens is recorded in the seventeenth chapter of the Book of Acts. While in Athens, Paul was greatly disturbed to see that the city was full of idols. Athens was, in fact, a city full of "higher powers," for there were dozens of gods in the Greek pantheon. Because he "was preaching the good news about Jesus and the resurrection" (Acts 17:18), Paul caught the attention of some of the local "philosophers." They invited him to speak at the Areopagus (sometimes called Ares' or Mars' Hill), a portion of the marketplace devoted solely to the debate of religious and ethical ideas.

Here, in the heart of pagan culture, Paul preached the Good News about Jesus! Notice Paul's courteous, diplomatic, and gentle manner as he addressed his pagan audience: "Men of Athens! I see that in every way you are very religious. For as I walked around and looked carefully at your objects of worship, I even found an altar with this inscription: TO AN UNKNOWN GOD. Now what you worship as something unknown I am going to proclaim to you" (Acts 17:22–23).

Three things are outstanding in Paul's address. First, he begins by complimenting the men of Athens ("I see that in every way you are very religious"). Second, he tells his audience that he has made a *careful* examination of their objects of worship. His was not a knee-jerk response to a religion that was strange and different from his own. He did not speak from ignorance nor attempt to hide a lack of understanding with ridicule, insult, or invective. Third, he used one of their religious shrines as the means to introduce the gospel of Jesus Christ. Further in his address, Paul even quoted one of the Greeks' own poets. As a starting point for his presentation of the gospel, Paul used objects and concepts already familiar to his audience.

The parallels are clear for those of us faced with the myriad higher powers found in Twelve-Step meetings. We are not to attack or ridicule those who seriously seek a higher power to restore them to sanity, even though that higher power is different from our own. Following the method of the Apostle Paul, we must seek to understand our fellow travelers in recovery so as to bridge the cultural/religious gap between us and make a way for a loving, caring presentation of the gospel of Jesus Christ. Bible pounding and soapbox preaching will alienate those who are in need of the saving power of Jesus Christ. However, we must not be naive regarding the various higher powers with which we are confronted; we must remember that we also struggle "against the spiritual forces of evil" (Eph. 6:12).

When the subject of the higher power arises at Twelve-Step meetings, I suggest that we Christians in recovery preface our remarks with the statement, "My Higher Power is Jesus Christ, and he tells me . . ." In so doing, we not only introduce the King of the Universe into the discussion, but also we provide the tacit implication that we are ready and willing to share the Good News about Jesus to anyone who wishes to listen.

As Christians in recovery we have the opportunity to share a unique kind of experience, strength, and hope that derives *only* from a personal relationship with Jesus Christ. He said:

> You are the light of the world. A city on a hill cannot be hidden. Neither do people light a lamp and put it under a bowl. Instead they put it on its stand, and it gives light to everyone in the house. In the same way, let your light shine before men, that they may see your good deeds and praise your Father in heaven. (Matt. 5:14–16)

A light's job is to shine. Its radiance is there for any who would come and share it. The light neither solicits nor discriminates; it attracts by its radiance. Like a city on a hill, shining its light for those travelers who would come to it, we must allow the light of the gospel of Jesus Christ to shine out of us so that whoever will may come to *the* Light.

CHAPTER V

Faith

STEP TWO: *Came to believe that a Power greater than ourselves could restore us to sanity.*

RELIEVE ME OF THE BONDAGE OF SELF

Jesus Christ is the only legitimate Higher Power; only he and he alone can restore us to sanity. Coming to believe in his ability and willingness to heal us is the central issue of Step Two.

As a prerequisite for the second step, we must acknowledge our inability to cease addictive behavior when left to our own devices. Bitter experience has shown us time and again that we cannot do it alone. The powerlessness and unmanageability at last admitted at Step One can only be overcome with the aid of one who is greater than ourselves, and that one is Jesus Christ.

The self-centered lifestyle of addiction does not die easily, however, even when a program of recovery is undertaken.

To dethrone self and enthrone Jesus Christ as the only legitimate ruler in our lives is not a quick and easy decision made some bright Sunday morning. The dethronement of self and the concomitant enthronement of the Lord Jesus Christ as the primary influence in our lives is an ongoing process, one that lasts a lifetime. Egocentricity dies hard. Just as we think we are finally "turning it over" to a Power greater than ourselves, our old, self-centered nature jumps back to center stage and takes the reins of our lives as we regress to old behaviors and gallop off in all four directions at once.

But not to worry. Recovery need not be—will not be—picture perfect. Recall Paul's words cited earlier and read them now in the context of Step Two: "I do not understand what I do. For what I want to do I do not do, but what I hate I do . . . For what I do is not the good I want to do; no, the evil I do not want to do—this I keep on doing" (Rom. 7:15, 19). Like the rest of us, Paul, too, struggled with his "old" egocentric nature. In formulating his thoughts on the solution to his dilemma, Paul embraced the heart of Step Two when he wrote, "What a wretched man I am! Who will rescue me from this body of death? Thanks be to God—through Jesus Christ our Lord!" (Rom. 7:24–25).

Paul knew that he could not do it alone. He knew well that a Power greater than himself was essential if he were to overcome the egocentric demands of his sinful nature. It is the submission to a Power greater than ourselves that slays the dragon of egocentricity and breaks the chains of self-centeredness. The recognition of our total dependence on God to break the chains of self-centeredness and to restore us to sanity is profoundly clear in *The Big Book of AA*: "Relieve me of the bondage of self, that I might better do Thy will."[1] It is God's liberating grace that frees us to turn to him for restoration and healing.

CAME TO BELIEVE

Faith is the bridge that spans the chasm between what is and what might be.

The statement "Came to believe that a Power greater than ourselves could restore us to sanity" introduces the concept of *faith* into the program of recovery. Step Two is sometimes referred to as "the step of faith." Just as faith is an essential component in the steps of salvation, so, too, it is an essential aspect of recovery from addiction.

Dr. Billy Graham identifies three aspects of faith: 1) knowledge (intellect), 2) emotion, and 3) will.[2] The first two aspects of faith are inherent in the phrase "Came to believe," and the third aspect is consequential to it. A successful program of recovery will encompass all three aspects of faith.

In our discussion of Step Two, we will address the intellectual and emotional aspects of faith, reserving the volitional aspect (will and actions) for Step Three.

A CHANGED MIND

The lifestyle of addiction is filled with hurt, guilt, sorrow, and the many other painful emotions we have tried to soothe with chemicals or compulsive behaviors. We recovering addicts, then, have special insight into Paul's words, "Godly sorrow brings repentance that leads to salvation and leaves no regret, but worldly sorrow brings death" (2 Cor. 7:10). Godly sorrow is genuine *remorse* over the chaos and pain suffered by ourselves and others as a result of our addictions. Worldly sorrow is regretting that we got caught!

As Paul states, Godly sorrow leads to repentance. "Repentance" comes from the Greek word *metanoia,* which means "a changing of the mind." Step Two is precisely that—a changing of the mind. We move from a state of unbelief to a state of belief—we "came to believe." It is in this sense that Paul writes in another place, "Do not conform any longer to the pattern of this world, but be transformed by the renewing of your mind. Then you will be able to test and approve what God's will is" (Rom. 12:2). Step Two is a renewal of the mind. Our thinking is transformed as we move from the egocentric, self-centered lifestyle of addiction to a lifestyle in which Jesus Christ is the center and Higher Power. As our thinking is transformed, as our minds are renewed, we become more focused on God's will for our lives.

The Necessity of a Transformed Mind

It is the plight of all unbelievers to be alienated and cut off from God, the wellspring of life. Until they begin the process of recovery, those trapped in the chaotic lifestyle of prolonged addiction are no exception.

The progressive degradation in lifestyle of those persons who are alienated from God is clearly evidenced in the first chapter of the Book of Romans. Although Paul is speaking of unbelievers in general, his words are clearly applicable to the downhill slide into immorality and depravity that frequently accompanies prolonged addiction. Speaking of those who are alienated from God, Paul says, "their thinking became futile and their foolish hearts were darkened." Paul continues, "Although they claimed to be wise, they became fools." Later, he says, "since they did not think it worthwhile to retain the knowledge of God, he gave them over to a depraved mind" (Rom. 1:21–22, 28).

"Their thinking became futile" or ineffective and useless. Their minds were "depraved." This progressive degradation in their thinking results in "every kind of wickedness, evil, greed and depravity" (Rom. 1:29). A down-the-gutter spiral ensues when the mind is centered on self rather than God. No wonder the old-timers in Twelve-Step meetings repeatedly warn against "stinking thinking." Like Paul, they know very well that that kind of thinking takes us down the tubes! Part of the inherent wisdom of the Twelve Steps is that they ask for a transformation of the mind early in the program of recovery.

Insanity is the appropriate word for the lifestyle described by Paul in the opening passages of Romans. *Insanity* describes the moral and behavioral results of the human mind cut off from the Holy Spirit of God. *Insanity* also appropriately describes the chaotic lifestyle of years of runaway addiction. The mind not renewed with the Spirit of God is insane and at odds with God. Paul said, "the sinful mind is hostile to God" (Rom. 8:7).

Sanity, however, is characteristic of the mind imbued with God's spirit. The changing of the mind called for in Step Two ("came to believe") is a prerequisite for a restoration to sanity. AA literature sometimes describes sanity as "soundness of mind." For the Christian in recovery, this description is appropriate, for "God has not given us a spirit of fear, but of power and of love and of a sound mind" (2 Tim. 1:7, New King James Version). The furthest reach of sanity or soundness of mind is a mind imbued with and directed by the Spirit of God and focused on Jesus Christ.

TRUST

The phrase "came to believe" implies more, however, than just a changed mind, for the second step addresses a kind of faith that is more than mere "head knowledge." Implied in the second step is the essential, vital element of *trust.* In taking Step Two, we put our trust in a higher power; we acknowledge our total dependence on him to restore us to sanity. We stop trying to do it all ourselves; we stop trying to figure it all out. Instead, we place our trust in God to restore us. Thus "head knowledge" becomes "heart knowledge."

Abraham

To help us understand that the faith required in the second step is more than a mere intellectual belief, let us consider the paragon of faith—Abraham, the father of the faithful.

The Book of Genesis tells us that Abram (Abraham) lived in a city called Haran. He was a man of considerable wealth. His household and inheritance consisted of numerous relatives, servants, flocks, and other material possessions. Doubtless, Abram was a man of social and political influence as well.

One day, God interrupted Abram's confortable existence by instructing him to leave his home in Haran and go to a land that God would show him (*see* Gen. 12:1). God promised Abram a new homeland where his descendants would multiply and become a great nation. (It is important to note that Abram was 75 years old at the time, and he and his wife Sarah had no children.) Later, God reemphasized his promise by stating that Abram's descendants would be as numerous and uncountable as the stars of heaven (*see* Gen. 15:5).

Looking back from the vantage point of 18 centuries later, the writer of Hebrews tells us:

> By faith Abraham, when called to go to a place he would later receive as his inheritance, obeyed and went, even though he did not know where he was going . . . By faith Abraham, even though he was past age—and Sarah herself was barren—was enabled to become a father because he considered him

> [God] faithful who had made the promise. And so from this one man, and he as good as dead, came descendants as numerous as the stars in the sky and as countless as the sand on the seashore. (Heb. 11:8, 11–12)

In many ways, recovery is an Abraham-like experience. From the rock-bottom powerlessness of Step One, we are invited to believe, like Abraham, that God, a Power greater than ourselves, will lead us from powerlessness and unmanageability to sanity. But like Abraham, when we set out on the journey of recovery we have no idea where we are going.

The important point for us in the previous passage is that Abraham "considered" God "faithful." In other words, Abraham believed that God would keep his promises. Abraham trusted God to take care of him. It is not for great accomplishments, deeds, or works that Abraham is remembered, though doubtless, there were many of these; Abraham is remembered for his faith!

> What does the Scripture say? "Abraham believed God, and it was credited to him as righteousness." . . . he did not waver through unbelief regarding the promise of God, but was strengthened in his faith and gave glory to God, being fully persuaded that God had power to do what he had promised. This is why "it was credited to him as righteousness." (Rom. 4:3, 20–22)

Abraham is the model for faith. He "believed" God's promise regarding a son even though he and his wife were very old; he was "fully persuaded" that God had the power and faithfulness to do what he had promised Abraham. When God said, "Get up and go," Abraham got up and went! That is *faith*! And that is what was "credited" to Abraham as "righteousness." The writer of Hebrews defines this kind of faith as "being sure of what we hope for and certain of what we do not see" (Heb. 11:1).

Clearly, Abraham's faith involved more than a mere intellectual assent to God's promises. Not only did he believe God, Abraham trusted God. In fact, Abraham so trusted God that he willingly left the familiar comforts of family, friends, and country to travel to a distant and unknown land—one that God would show him only after he had left his homeland (*see* Heb. 11:8). Thus Abraham entrusted himself and all he had to God!

Biblical faith cannot be understood in the absence of the essential element of trust. As Christians in recovery, we must not only *believe* in Jesus Christ, but also we must entrust our lives and well-being to him in much the same way that Abraham entrusted all to God.

For Christians in recovery, the absolute necessity of trusting God becomes painfully clear when we admit our powerlessness over addiction. Our innumerable attempts to restore ourselves to sanity have demonstrated conclusively that we are unable to save ourselves. Our only recourse is to trust the Higher Power to restore us to sanity. Steps One and Two acknowledge both our inability to save ourselves and our complete dependence on God to restore us. At Step Two, our task is simply to trust God to heal us. In the next Step, we act on that trust.

RESTORE US TO SANITY

Step Two may be viewed not only as the step of faith, but also as the step of restoration. There is a profound truth that underlies this step—the truth that God himself wishes to restore the relationship between him and us!

The relationship between God and humanity was disrupted by sin. Sin, whether personal sin or the sinful nature that plagues us all, has separated us from God (*see* Isa. 59:2). The way to Eden has been blocked by a flaming sword (*see* Gen. 3:24). In our unsaved state, we are alienated or cut off from God. We are like blind people lost in a strange place; we cannot find our way. The path to God is blocked by the wall of sin that separates us.

Step Two is possible because God himself has taken the initiative in restoring the relationship between us and him. By sending his son Jesus Christ to pay the penalty for our sins, God has torn down the wall that separated us from him. Restoring the relationship between God and humankind is now possible because of what he has done. He has graciously taken the initiative to restore us. We respond to his initiative in faith, trusting that he has done everything necessary to restore and heal the once-broken relationship between us. Upon our response in faith to what he has done, we are declared "right with God." We are justified in his sight and totally acceptable to him.

> Therefore, since we have been justified through faith, we have peace with God through our Lord Jesus Christ, through whom we have gained access by faith into this grace in which we now stand. (Rom 5:1–2a)

FROM STEP TWO TO STEP THREE

As mentioned previously, faith has another aspect in addition to its intellectual and emotional aspects. The godly sorrow that leads to repentance leads not only to a changed mind but also to a changed lifestyle. Trusting faith leads to action.

At this point we are faced with the volitional aspect of faith—*will*. As we think of will, the next step in the program of recovery emerges into view, for it is in the third step that we must decide what to do with our will.

In Step Two, we come to God in faith; we come to believe that a Power greater than ourselves can restore us to sanity. As Christians, we have come to believe that Jesus Christ will restore us—mentally, emotionally, and spiritually. Now we come to the step where we must *act* on our faith and demonstrate our trust.

Billy Graham tells a story that beautifully illustrates how faith necessarily entails trust, which is needed as we move beyond the belief of Step Two into the commitment of Step Three. To paraphrase the story: A brave man pushes a wheelbarrow back and forth along a tightrope suspended high above Niagara Falls. The crowd watches in astonishment as the agile acrobat continues to push the wheelbarrow back and forth over the deadly, roaring falls. Then the man places a 200-pound sack of dirt in the wheelbarrow and boldly makes his way across the falls, pushing the heavy load through the misty air. Making his way back, the tightrope walker points to a man in the crowd and asks, "Do you believe I can push a man in the wheelbarrow across the falls?" The excited onlooker says, "Yes, of course." The acrobat points directly at the man and says, "Get in!"[3] Step Three is about getting into the wheelbarrow.

God As We Understand Him

STEP THREE: *Made a decision to turn our will and our lives over to the care of God* as we understood Him.

The transformation of our thinking called for in Step Two is a prerequisite to the spiritual decision and concomitant action of Step Three. Real *faith* is needed to get into the wheelbarrow. However, before we consider the vital notion of "turning it over to God," let's consider that portion of Step Three that addresses God "as we understand Him."

For many who practice the Twelve Steps, myself included, Step Three is the heart of the program. For many in recovery, this step has been the gateway through which they embarked on the pathway to God. For others, Step Three has been the means by which they were able to cease running from God and find their way back to the loving Father who was patiently awaiting their return.

Yet a consideration of God "as we understand Him" must include the dimmer side of this concept, namely, God "as we do not understand him." Assuredly, there is more about God that escapes our understanding than is comprehended by our finite minds. In fact, God is *beyond* our understanding; he is larger than our understanding! The very name "God" diminishes the being we are attempting to comprehend when we ascribe this or any other name to him. To name him is to reduce him. He is beyond our ability to create adequate descriptors for him. He is the Ineffable, the Unnameable One.

Psychologist and theologian Dr. Kenneth Gilburth states that the earliest Hebrews had no name for God. For them, God was so sacred and awesome that to assign him a name was irreverent. Rather than using a name, they paused "four beats" in the conversation. This reverent pause indicated that the speaker was referring to the Unnameable One. For example, "In the beginning (____________) created the heavens and the earth." As time passed, someone suggested they pick four letters that had no particular meaning and use them to represent (____________). Thus, God was given the name *YHWH,* which we pronounce Yahweh or, in anglicized form, Jehovah. From that point forward, states Dr. Gilburth, there has been a "progressive degradation" of the name of God so that today, it is frequently reduced to nothing more than a prefix for "dammit."

Assuredly, all our concepts of God are too small; all our names for him are inadequate; he is beyond our ability to conceive him. The finite is incapable of adequately conceiving the Infinite.

When we attempt to conceive the Majestic Unnameable One, we use concepts that are beyond our ability to adequately grasp. We ascribe to God such adjectives as omnipotent (all-powerful), omniscient (all-knowing), and omnipresent (everywhere at once). Cynics attack us by asking, "If God is all-powerful, can he make a rock so big that he can't lift it?" (God "loses" either way, so they think.) I certainly cannot answer that question. Can you? It seems there are things about God that our minds can't figure out! That doesn't mean God is limited—it means we are.

Another example of our limited ability to conceive God is in the use of pronouns that refer to him. In this book, I refer to God as "he." Yet, God is neither male nor female; he is beyond the limitations of gender. God is spirit (*see* John 4.24).

In short, our conceptions of God are limited because of the limited abilities of our finite minds. Paul said, "Now we see but a poor reflection as in a mirror; then [in heaven] we shall see face to face. Now I know in part; then I shall know fully, even as I am fully known" (1 Cor. 13:12).

There is more to God than meets the eye. He is greater, more magnificent, more powerful, more unspeakable, and more loving than we are capable of imagining. (I suggest you read Job 38:1–42:6 in regard to the present subject matter.)

How is it possible, then, to *understand* God? We can understand God because *he* has made himself known to us, albeit in a manner scaled down to our size. God has made himself known to us in three ways: 1) general revelation, 2) special revelation, and 3) incarnation.

GENERAL AND SPECIAL REVELATION

When theologians speak of "general revelation," they are referring to nature or the created universe. The creation itself shouts its witness to the Creator:

> The heavens declare the glory of God;
> the skies proclaim the work of his hands.
> Day after day they pour forth speech;
> night after night they display knowledge.

> There is no speech or language
> where their voice is not heard.
> Their voice goes out into all the earth,
> their words to the ends of the world. (Ps. 19:1–4)

Who has not looked spellbound into the heavens on a cold, clear, starry night and wondered in awe at the celestial witness of God? From the intricate patterns of orbiting electrons to the timely, orderly orbiting of planets in innumerable solar systems, the creation proclaims the glory of its Creator!

Paul states that "since the creation of the world God's invisible qualities—his eternal power and divine nature—have been clearly seen, being understood from what has been made, so that men are without excuse" (Rom. 1:20). Throughout the ages, people in every tribe, culture, and nation have sought God because of the witness of his creation. It is as natural for a human being to seek God as for a thirsty deer to seek water.

Left to our own devices, however, the trail we follow to God may be a false one. Paul continues:

> For although they knew God, they neither glorified him as God nor gave thanks to him, but their thinking became futile and their foolish hearts were darkened. Although they claimed to be wise, they became fools and exchanged the glory of the immortal God for images made to look like mortal man and birds and animals and reptiles. (Rom. 1:21–23)

These verses describe the decline into idolatry of those who wish to reduce God to more "manageable" proportions. Because of humankind's proclivity to pervert its innate need for God into idolatry, there are many idols in the world, not all of which are made of wood or stone or look like birds, animals, or reptiles. Ours is a culture given to the idolatry of materialism. Our idols are more likely to be made of chrome, porcelain, or microchips. Instead of gawking eyes of rubies or emeralds, they more likely will exhibit pulsating lights and flashing LEDs.

Our culture also exhibits an alarming tendency toward an idolatry involving addictive chemicals. Making idols of addictive chemicals (or even compulsive behaviors) is part of the downhill slide into addiction, both on a personal and a cultural level. The importance attached to the addictive chemical or behavior is nothing less than idolatrous.

Because of our tendency to get sidetracked into idolatry, something else is needed to keep us on the right path to God and out of the clutches of the false gods lurking beside that path; that "something" is special revelation.

By *special revelation,* theologians mean specifically "the word of God written," that is, the Holy Bible. The written word of God is essential to an "understanding" of the Creator and Ruler of the Universe. Further, the Holy Bible acts as a trustworthy map for guiding our lives, as the following verses indicate:

> All Scripture is God-breathed and is useful for teaching, rebuking, correcting and training in righteousness, so that the man of God may be thoroughly equipped for every good work. (2 Tim. 3:16–17)

> For the word of God is living and active. Sharper than any double-edged sword, it penetrates even to dividing soul and spirit, joints and marrow; it judges the thoughts and attitudes of the heart. (Heb. 4:12)

Moreover, it is in God's word, the Holy Bible, that we find the biographical account of the life of Jesus Christ. The Gospels (Matthew, Mark, Luke, and John) are the greatest repositories of the deeds and teachings of Jesus. As Christians in recovery, we are personally responsible for studying the life and teachings of our Lord. It is *not* enough to leave it to the preachers and theologians to tell us about the life and teachings of Jesus. The Apostle Paul would not have it so; he personally commended the Christians in Berea because they "examined the Scriptures every day to see if what Paul said was true" (Acts 17:11). By studying for ourselves the life of our Lord as revealed in the Holy Bible, we expose ourselves to the historical miracle by which God may most clearly be understood—the incarnation.

INCARNATION

Incarnation means "enfleshment" or specifically, "God in the flesh." The most remarkable, awesome means of comprehending the ingenious phrase, "God as we understood him," is to understand that God has come to us. An understanding of God is ultimately possible only because *God* himself made it possible—and he did it for us by *revealing himself* to us in the flesh-and-blood personage of Jesus Christ. Paul describes it this way:

> Your attitude should be the same as that of Christ Jesus: Who, being in very nature God, did not consider equality with God something to be grasped, but made himself nothing, taking the very nature of a servant, being made in human likeness. And being found in appearance as a man, he humbled himself and became obedient to death—even death on a cross! (Phil. 2:5–8)

The Apostle John writes:

> In the beginning was the Word, and the Word was with God, and the Word was God . . . The Word became flesh and made his dwelling among us. (John 1:1, 14)

Citing an ancient prophecy about Jesus, Matthew wrote:

> "The virgin will be with child and will give birth to a son, and they will call him Immanuel"—which means, "God with us." (Matt. 1:23)

The incomprehensible reality, trumpeted throughout all Christendom, is that God became man!

Many, however, refuse to accept the historical fact that God became man. They prefer to reduce Jesus to the level of a wise sage or simply a nice guy. Skeptics who fail to recognize the historicalness of the incarnation, yet recognize the difficulty of finite man comprehending the Infinite God, declare that God—even if he exists—is so vastly superior to mere mortals that a relationship with him is both impossible and inconceivable.

In many eastern forms of religion, Hinduism for example, it is man who must find his way to God. Various means such as yoga and meditation are used to try to connect with God. Converts to new-age religions have adopted eastern techniques in an attempt to become "one" with God or to "meld with the universal consciousness."

Christianity, on the other hand, heralds the message that exotic means for finding God are *not* necessary. It is the central message of Christianity that people need not go and seek God because *God* has sought and found humankind! In other words, we need not, through our own efforts, seek to bridge the gap between ourselves and God; that gulf was bridged by *God* himself when he became man and gave himself for us. We can know God because *God has made himself known* in the person of the human being, Jesus of Nazareth; "He is the image of the invisible God" (Col. 1:15).

For the Christian in recovery, the phrase "God as we understand him" implies a personal, knowledgeable relationship with Jesus Christ. To "understand" God, we must understand Jesus. Through the incarnation, God "scaled himself down" to our size so that we could comprehend him, albeit to a limited degree.

The full glory and majesty of God is, of course, beyond our ability to comprehend or behold. When God walked this earth as the man Jesus of Nazareth, his glory was veiled or contained. On one occasion, however, Jesus Christ, God in the flesh, allowed some of his majestic glory to shine through:

> Jesus took with him Peter, James and John the brother of James, and led them up a high mountain by themselves. There he was transfigured before them. His face shone like the sun, and his clothes became as white as the light. Just then there appeared before them Moses and Elijah, talking with Jesus . . . a bright cloud enveloped them, and a voice from the cloud said, "This is my son, whom I love; with him I am well pleased. Listen to him." When the disciples heard this, they fell face down to the ground, terrified. (Matt. 17:1–6)

The momentary sight of Jesus, face shining like the sun, clothes as bright as the light; the appearance of the great leader Moses and the legendary prophet Elijah; a heavenly voice speaking from a cloud—overwhelmed the disciples; they were terrified! Yet this scene, so traumatic for the disciples, is commonplace in heaven from where Jesus descended. Routine events in heaven are overwhelming to the earthbound. Therefore, when God became flesh, he had to, let's say, turn down the rheostat of his majestic power to a level that could be contained by our limited ability to comprehend. God enabled us to understand him by becoming one of us—by descending to our level. He emptied himself of his heavenly glory and took "the very nature of a servant, being made in human likeness" (Phil. 2:7).

Jesus said, "Anyone who has seen me has seen the Father" (John 14:9). Therefore, it is incumbent upon recovering Christians grappling with Step Three to become knowledgeable of the person and life of Jesus Christ. It is in coming to an understanding of him that we come to an understanding of God. We must study for ourselves the life and teachings of the Lord Jesus Christ. He said:

> I am the way and the truth and the life. No one comes to the Father except through me. (John 14:6)

There is no doorway to salvation but Jesus. There is no legitimate higher power but Jesus. Only Jesus can restore us to sanity. This is why we must say and believe, "My Higher Power is Jesus Christ."

Does this imply, then, that there is only one way to understand Jesus? Must we all see him in the exact same light? Are our opinions of him to be exactly the same? Should all of us follow Jesus in exactly the same way? By no means! Jesus is the doorway through which we must pass to enter eternal life, yet we reach that doorway via many differing paths carved by infinite combinations of personality, upbringing, and life experiences.

Herein is, for me, the true meaning of the phrase "God as we understand him." Jesus is the God of whom the third step speaks; our understanding of Jesus, however, is intimate and *personal.* My understanding of the Lord Jesus Christ will be a bit different from yours. The central issue is the God who is being understood, not the person attempting to understand. The figure of central importance is Jesus Christ, not you nor I. Each of us is responsible for our understanding of Jesus. There are not many Jesuses; there is only one Lord Jesus Christ (*see* 1 Cor. 8:6). Jesus does not vary; he is "the same yesterday and today and forever" (Heb. 13:8). The variations lay in the perceivers—you and me—not in that which is perceived. It is essential, then, that we serve the Lord as we understand him.

MATTERS OF CONSCIENCE

Is it possible for two Christians who both earnestly seek to serve the Lord Jesus to do so in such a way that each may disagree with the other's method? Emphatically yes! Two servants of the Lord may serve him very differently, yet each differing manner of service is proper so long as it is offered in good *conscience.*

The Apostle Paul addresses the matter of "conscience" in 1 Corinthians, chapter 8. In the church at Corinth there was disagreement among Christians as to whether it was acceptable to eat meat that had been used in pagan religious services and subsequently sold at the local meat market. The meat could even show up as the main course at a feast where Christians were the invited guests. Some Corinthian Christians believed that to eat such meat was to make oneself a party to idol worship; others saw nothing wrong with eating the meat.

Who was right? Was it those who said abstain or those who said eat? If you were in that situation, which side would you choose? How would you feel about those on the other side? The answer is that *both* groups were right so long as each member of either group followed the dictates of individual conscience. It was perfectly acceptable for those who saw nothing wrong with the meat to eat it. On the other hand, for those who felt it was wrong to eat the meat, their consciences were "defiled" if they ate it because these Christians believed that to eat such meat was a sin against Christ. Thus we have two groups engaging in very different behaviors, yet both groups are still Christians and they still serve the same Lord. Paul summarized the matter by saying, "food does not bring us near to God; we are no worse if we do not eat and no better if we do" (1 Cor. 8:8).

Disagreements over mundane matters such as dietary considerations must have been common in the early Church because Paul had to address the matter again in his letter to the church at Rome. In that letter he stated that "if anyone regards something as unclean, then for him it is unclean" (Rom. 14:14).

Paul demonstrates clearly that there is ample room for individual differences in God's Church. And how could it be otherwise when we consider the widely varied backgrounds from which these early Christians came? Those Church members whose backgrounds were rooted in Judaism were accustomed to a religion replete with rules and regulations about every form of human behavior, including what to eat and what not to eat. These early Jewish Christians came from an oppressive religion that restricted virtually every aspect of their daily existence. Other members of the early Church came from backgrounds rooted in paganism, where drunkenness and debauchery were standard fare in their religious practices. The Greeks, for example, got drunk with the blessing of Bacchus, the god of wine, while partaking of temple prostitutes with the blessing of the goddess Aphrodite.

Naturally, these disparate backgrounds contributed to innumerable opinions regarding the "right" way to be a Christian. Imagine a black-coated, stiff-shirted, self-denying religious fanatic and a gold-chained, open-shirted, Ferrari-driving playboy—both newly converted to Christianity—trying to start a new church! Can you imagine their vast differences in opinion on how things should be done? Such must have been the difficulties faced by that motley group of early Christians as they earnestly sought to serve the Lord Jesus Christ. In his many letters to these Christians, Paul makes it clear that differences in opinion and behavior are not only to be expected, but also are to be tolerated.

Look at the contemporary Christian Church. Our worship services range from the emotional freedom of the Charismatics to the intellectual precision of the Calvinists. There are disparities in hairstyles as well as disagreements over the use of cosmetics. Some churches condemn divorce, categorizing it in close proximity to the "unpardonable sin"; other churches hold a lenient view of divorce. Some denominations ordain women into the ministry; others find no biblical support for the practice. While most Christian churches hold worship services on Sundays, some worship on Saturdays. Some churches condemn movies and card playing while others offer bingo on Wednesday nights. Baptists decry alcohol and Episcopalians use it in Communion. Who is right? Who is wrong? How is it possible for so many churches with such varying practices to claim to worship and serve the same Lord Jesus Christ?

I am thoroughly convinced that the variations in today's Christian beliefs and behaviors are largely attributable to differences in personalities, cognitive styles, and most of all, environmental experiences associated with upbringing. It is likely that most Baptists are Baptists and most Methodists are Methodists because their parents were. The same can be said of other denominations.

There are other variables contributing to differences in religious practices, of course. A highly cognitive, intellectual, nonemotional professional person would likely be uncomfortable in a Charismatic service marked by tinkling tambourines, waving arms, shouts of "amen," and speaking in tongues. Certain personality types tend to be attracted to certain types of services.

It is rare, unfortunately, for a person to "search the Scriptures" and make a biblically based decision as to which church or denomination is acting in closest accord to his or her understanding of biblical teachings. Usually, we choose the church where our parents go. (Sometimes we choose a church because our parents don't go there!) Or perhaps we go to the church that is attended by our friends. Sometimes we try different churches and stay with the one that "feels" right. In short, there is an infinite number of variables that interact in our choosing the church or denomination that is right for us.

A big problem arises, however, when some Christian groups get the notion that they are "right" and everyone else is "wrong." One group offers a highly trained doctor of theology to support its beliefs. Another dissenting group offers its own equally qualified scholar to support its beliefs. So long as the disagreements are friendly, no serious problems develop. When one group says, however, "We've got it and everyone else is going to hell!" then serious divisions occur. Those hostile to Christianity gloat over the internecine dissension and the Lord of us all, Jesus Christ, is greatly dishonored.

Christianity is an *inclusive* religion. It does not seek to exclude those on the "outside." The in-group/out-group mentality misses the point:

> For God so loved the world that he gave his one and only Son, that whoever believes in him shall not perish but have eternal life. (John 3:16)

JESUS OUR HIGH PRIEST

Jesus is the way—not the group, not a church, not the institution called the Church. Because Jesus is our High Priest, each of us has a *direct* line, through prayer, to him. Jesus acts as our advocate, interceding on our behalf with the heavenly Father:

> Therefore, since we have a great high priest who has gone through the heavens, Jesus the Son of God, let us hold firmly to the faith we profess. For we do not have a high priest who is unable to sympathize with our weaknesses, but we have one who has been tempted in every way, just as we are—yet was without sin. Let us then approach the throne of grace with confidence, so that we may receive mercy and find grace to help us in our time of need. (Heb. 4:14–16)

Each of us may "approach the throne of grace with confidence" because Jesus himself has paid the penalty for our sins and is in heaven interceding on our behalf. No other person or institution is needed for us to have a personal relationship with the Risen Lord.

As each of us seeks individually to ascertain God's will in our lives, choices and actions will be monitored by the dictates of individual conscience. Some will dress in ways that others deem inappropriate. Some will watch movies or frequent establishments that others think sinful. One will engage in dietary habits that another finds distasteful. Some (not recovering chemical dependents) will consume alcohol; others will deem drinking sinful. Some Christians will enter the doorway of the church every time it opens; others will worship as they behold a sunrise on a remote mountain lake some beautiful Sunday morning.

As we enjoy the liberty that God has granted us, however, we must be careful how we use it. Paul warns us clearly not to use our freedom to offend another Christian; nor are we to use our freedom to tempt a brother or sister in Christ to do anything his or her conscience dictates as wrong (*see* 1 Cor. 8 and Rom. 14). Those who see things differently are entitled to their opinions because they, too, have been bought with the blood of Jesus.

> You, then, why do you judge your brother? Or why do you look down on your brother? For we will all stand before God's judgment seat . . . So then, each of us will give an account of himself to God. Therefore let us stop passing judgment on one another. Instead, make up your mind not to put any stumbling block or obstacle in your brother's way. (Rom. 14:10, 12–13)

There is wide latitude and great freedom in the phrase "God as we understand him." For the recovering Christian, that "God" is the Lord Jesus Christ; "as we understand him" is the product of the interaction of personality, upbringing, and life experience (included in "life experience" is time spent searching the Scriptures and using study aids as we strive to "grow in the grace and knowledge of our Lord and Savior Jesus Christ" [2 Pet. 3:18]).

Jesus Christ is like a multifaceted, priceless jewel. That jewel can be viewed from many angles and perspectives, yet always remains beautiful, regardless of the point of view from which it is beheld. The various churches and denominations behold the multifaceted beauty of the Lord from differing points of view; nevertheless, he is the same Lord, the same jewel of infinite worth. For the Christian in recovery, the third step is an acknowledgment of the multifaceted beauty of God as well as the many perspectives from which he can be understood.

GOD AS WE MISUNDERSTAND HIM

Given the wide latitude and freedom implicit in the phrase "God as we understand him," a more restrictive and spiritually crippling effect arises from our *mis*understandings of God. All too frequently, our perceptions of God are twisted and distorted. These misperceptions often result from early life experiences, especially those social interactions involving parents and significant others.

It is not uncommon for chemically dependent people and other addicts to come from dysfunctional families. Mental health professionals have noted repeatedly that children with one or more alcoholic parents are at increased risk for developing alcoholism. As this knowledge increases, there is a growing awareness of the great similarities in the cognitive, emotional, and behavioral characteristics of adults who grew up in dysfunctional families. Whether the adult child comes from a family where there was parental alcoholism, workaholism, mental illness, rigid religiosity, or numerous other forms of parental dysfunction, the effects upon family members are similar.

One of the effects of parental dysfunction as experienced by adult children is twisted and distorted *mis*conceptions about God. In her research with Christian adult children of alcoholics, Dr. Sandra D. Wilson identified "five major distortions of the character of God common to Christian adult children of alcoholics." These include 1) the cruel and capricious God, 2) the demanding and unforgiving God, 3) the selective and unfair God, 4) the distant and unavailable God, and 5) the kind but confused God.[1]

These distortions of the character of God derive directly from painful childhood experiences with parents and significant others. For example, the "cruel and capricious God" is the distorted concept held by those who were repeatedly abused as children. Included among these adult children are victims of both sexual abuse and physical abuse. For these children, one or both parents were cruel and unpredictable.

The cruelty they experienced at the hands of an abusive parent is generalized to God. At a largely subconscious level, they perceive God as having the same characteristics of cruelty and capriciousness as the abusive parent. In a similar fashion, the other distortions of the character of God held by Christian adult children of alcoholics began with early, painful childhood experiences with adults.

Distorted concepts of God are not the only way in which an adult's spirituality could have been affected by parental dysfunction. Dr. Wilson's research reveals that evangelical adult children of alcoholics differ from evangelical adults from nonalcoholic homes in their "religious perceptions." She categorized religious perceptions in four ways: 1) experiencing God's love and forgiveness, 2) trusting God's will, 3) believing biblical promises regarding God's care, and 4) extending forgiveness to others. Her research revealed that adults raised in dysfunctional families have difficulty in personally experiencing the love and forgiveness of God. They have difficulty trusting God or believing the Scriptures that pertain to God's promise to love and care for us. Not surprisingly, they have difficulty forgiving others.[2]

Dr. Wilson's finding that adult children of alcoholics have difficulty "believing biblical promises regarding God's care" is especially relevant to Step Three, because it invites recovering Christians to turn their will and lives over to the *care* of God.

Many recovering Christians will identify with the distorted concepts of God described by Dr. Wilson. The distortions in "religious perceptions" will likely seem quite familiar as well.

The problem is that our "understanding" of God is confused by the painful, often abusive, experiences of childhood. If our parents were impossible to please, unforgiving, and overly demanding, we will have a strong tendency to view God in the same manner. From the child's point of view, parents were the first "all-powerful, all-knowing" beings with whom we had experience. An inevitable, unconscious process generalizes their faults to the all-powerful, all-knowing God of heaven. Painful and abusive experiences with other important people in our lives—teachers, coaches, Sunday school teachers, relatives—only make matters worse.

It is essential for Christians in recovery to seek scriptural and other spiritual guidance to disentangle our twisted perceptions of God so we can experience the love, kindness, and forgiveness of the God who is defined as love (*see* 1 John 4:16b).

CORRECTING DISTORTIONS

An especially good place to begin experiencing the love of our heavenly Father is the short letter in the New Testament called 1 John. This epistle was written by John, the one of the twelve disciples who was especially close to Jesus. Part of John's purpose in writing this letter to early Christians was to reveal the tremendous love God has for us. He writes:

> How great is the love the Father has lavished on us, that we should be called children of God! (1 John 3:1)

Notice that God has "lavished" his love on us. To *lavish* means to bestow liberally, generously, and abundantly. God has not been stingy with his love for us; he has offered it liberally and freely.

John also writes:

> This is how God showed his love among us: He sent his one and only Son into the world that we might live through him.

> This is love: not that we loved God, but that he loved us and sent his Son as an atoning sacrifice for our sins. Dear friends, since God so loved us, we also ought to love one another. (1 John 4:9–11)

The word *love* appears numerous times throughout 1 John. The theme of love, especially God's love for us, is woven throughout the epistle like a thread of gold in a fine tapestry:

> God is love. Whoever lives in love lives in God, and God in him . . . There is no fear in love. But perfect love drives out fear, because fear has to do with punishment . . . We love because he first loved us. (1 John 4:16–19)

I would be remiss if I failed to remind the reader of another passage written many years earlier by John. This one is often quoted but too little appreciated:

> For God so loved the world that he gave his one and only Son, that whoever believes in him shall not perish but have eternal life. (John 3:16)

How different the God revealed in these love-filled passages than the harsh, critical, judgmental, and angry god so often misconceived by addicts struggling with the third step.

Notice what God did. He loved the world. He gave his only Son, Jesus. No wonder this particular passage (John 3:16) appears on so many signs and banners at major sporting events. These well-intentioned sign makers are attempting to convey in the most succinct terms possible the central message of Scripture from Genesis to Revelation—that God loves you! In fact, God loves you so much that he sent his Son to die for you, to pay the price for your sins, and to make it possible for you to live with him forever.

Still, I can sense the jaws grinding in the heads of some readers now as images of that harsh, judgmental God creep back in. "But what about my sins?" you think. "You just don't know how rotten I've been!" Or perhaps you've heard some fire-and-brimstone self-proclaimed evangelist, leering from an orange-crate pulpit, shriek out invectives about God's justice and wrath! Yes, God is just. And he can be wrathful with those who repeatedly refuse to follow the path of love, choosing rather to follow the path of hate or greed or injustice.

Scripture makes it clear that the penalty for breaking God's law is death (*see* Rom. 6:23). In his holiness and justness, God has the right to exact the death penalty for the transgression of his law. In his mercy and love, however, God chose to pay that just penalty *for* us. Here, then, is the purpose of the incarnation and subsequent death of Jesus Christ: God's justice was satisfied by the substitutionary death of his Son on the cross; on that same cross, God's unspeakable love for us was manifested—Jesus Christ, God in the flesh, paid the penalty of death for us, for you and for me. No wonder they call it the "Good News"!

Now, let's look at another passage that may help to dispel all remaining distortions of the God who is love.

The Prodigal Son

The New International Version of the Bible refers to this passage as "The Parable of the Lost Son." It could just as easily be described as "The Parable of the Lost Daughter." Perhaps a better title, however, is "The Parable of the Forgiving Father." This famous story was told by Jesus himself and is recorded in the Gospel of Luke, chapter 15. I urge you to take the time to read this parable before going further.

In the story, the younger of two sons asked his father for his inheritance. The boy probably said something like, "Give it to me now, Dad; I don't want to wait till you're dead. I'll be too old to enjoy it then!" Who knows, this son may have been a practicing chemical dependent himself; like so many of us, he had trouble delaying gratification. So the father gave the younger son his portion of the inheritance.

"Not long after that, the younger son got together all he had, set off for a distant country and there squandered his wealth in wild living" (Luke 15:13). (Sounds like an addict to me!) Flat broke and busted, this wild and crazy young son ended up slopping hogs for a local farmer.

Think about it—a young Jew slopping hogs (pork) for a Gentile farmer. Talk about rock bottom; he was as low as he could go. "He longed to fill his stomach with the pods that the pigs were eating, but no one gave him anything" (Luke 15:16).

It is at this rock-bottom place that "he came to his senses" (Luke 15:17). Just as Joseph began to wake up while at the bottom of the well, the Prodigal Son came to his senses in the hog pen. Frequently, it takes the crash at the bottom of the elevator shaft to turn the addict around.

After coming to his senses, the wayward younger son decided to return to his father. Apparently this formerly know-it-all, shiny-faced lad had learned a lesson. His egocentricity or self-centeredness was left behind in the muck and mire of the hog pen. He started toward home, intending to seek employment as a hired hand because he no longer considered himself worthy to be called his father's son.

> So he got up and went to his father. But while he was still a long way off, his father saw him and was filled with compassion for him; he ran to his son, threw his arms around him and kissed him. (Luke 15:20)

Notice that the father was *not* standing on the porch with stern face and furrowed brow, arms crossed, foot tapping impatiently as he watched his wealth-squandering younger son approaching. Instead, the father *ran* to his son! Imagine this stately, dignified patriarch tugging at the skirt of his toga with his old, knobby, bare knees protruding and his sandals slapping the ground as he rushed to his son. This father did not stand still in righteous indignation as his son approached; instead, he showered him with hugs and kisses.

Biblical scholars are in wide agreement that Jesus clearly intended for the father in this story to represent the heavenly Father—God himself. The younger son represents you and me—sinners who have left the realm of the Father, squandered all manner of wealth, and wallowed in the muck and mire of addiction.

It is imperative that we understand what Jesus is teaching us with this story. He uses it to illustrate the tremendous love our heavenly Father has "lavished" on us. God does *not* stand before his throne with stern face and furrowed brow, arms crossed, foot tapping impatiently as he surveys the latest sins of his wayward children. Rather, God actively seeks out his children with open arms, anxiously awaiting our turning to him, eager to lavish his love on us. God is anxious to run to us, to meet us at far more than halfway, if only we will come to our senses and leave the hog pen.

As recovering Christians, we do not have to crawl back to God or come before his throne, hat in hand, hoping to receive crumbs from his table. But make no mistake—it is not because of anything we have done that God lavishes his love on us. We have squandered our wealth—wives, husbands, children, jobs, reputations—in the wild living so frequently characteristic of active addiction. God lavishes his love on us because he is a God of love and because he finds us infinitely lovable. This is what John means when he writes, "God is love." God runs, as it were, with open arms toward his children, even while we are "still a long way off."

Thus the Scripture says that "God demonstrates his own love for us in this: While we were still sinners, Christ died for us" (Rom. 5:8). God himself crossed the gulf that separated us. Jesus Christ is the bridge that connects us. God hastens across the bridge made by Jesus to welcome us home. He throws his arms around us and walks with us, arm in arm, as we return to the realm of our loving Father.

Jesus said, "I tell you that in the same way there will be more rejoicing in heaven over one sinner who repents than over ninety-nine righteous persons who do not need to repent" (Luke 15:7). In the parable of the lost son, the father says:

> "Quick! Bring the best robe and put it on him [the younger son]. Put a ring on his finger and sandals on his feet. Bring the fattened calf and kill it. Let's have a feast and celebrate. For this son of mine was dead and is alive again; he was lost and is found." (Luke 15:22–24)

God is ready to lavish his love upon us, to declare a celebration. There is joy in heaven when a recovering addict takes Step Three and turns it over to God.

CHAPTER VII

Getting into the Wheelbarrow

STEP THREE: *Made a decision to turn our will and our lives over to the care of God* as we understood Him.

Now we come to that portion of Step Three that addresses "our will and our lives." What does it mean when we state that we "made a decision to turn our will and our lives over to the care of God as we understood him"?

First, it is essential to note that we make a decision to *do* something. Some members of Twelve-Step programs mistakenly believe that Step Three is about simply making a decision, that is, coming to a particular state of mind. To the contrary, it is in Step Two that we come to a new state of mind, a transformation in our thinking. In Step Three, however, we go beyond a particular change of mind to a program of action—we make a decision to turn our will and our lives over to the care of God.

Recovery is an active process. Those of us in recovery are actively responsible for the management of our illnesses. Remember the story about the acrobat pushing the wheelbarrow across Niagara Falls? He challenged an onlooker to put his beliefs into action. It is one thing to believe the acrobat could push a man across the falls in a wheelbarrow; it is another thing to get in! The Apostle James wrote, "faith by itself, if it is not accompanied by action, is dead" (James 2:17). Therefore, the faith of Step Two must issue forth in the action of Step Three.

REPENTANCE—A CHANGE OF DIRECTION

In our discussion of Step Two, we saw that faith involves the intellect, the emotions, and the will (volition). The first two aspects of faith were discussed in Chapter 5. The latter aspect of faith, will, necessarily brings us to the biblical concept of *repentance.*

Like faith, repentance involves the mind and the emotions as well as the will. As stated earlier, repentance involves a changing of the mind, but it is more than that; repentance also includes the idea of *turning around,* literally a *change* in the *direction* of one's life. Repentance is like making a U-turn and going in the opposite direction. This is the point at which faith becomes *action.*

In the parable of the Prodigal Son discussed earlier, we saw that the Prodigal's life went downhill, all the way down into the hog pen. His repentance occurred when he "came to his senses" (a change of mind) and got up from the muck and mire to return to his father (action). He changed the direction of his life by making a complete about-face, turning 180 degrees from the course that led him to the hog pen.

Those trapped in active addiction are on a similar course—an elevator ride going down. Since the descending elevator of addiction eventually crashes at the bottom, it is vital that the direction of their lives change. Failure to turn around leads to death—mentally, emotionally, spiritually, and often physically. Like the Prodigal Son, recovering addicts must make a complete turnaround and return to the Heavenly Father. Such is the essence of repentance.

> For you have spent enough time in the past doing what pagans choose to do—living in debauchery, lust, drunkenness, orgies, carousing and detestable idolatry. (1 Pet. 4:3)

Many of us who spent years trapped in addiction lived down to the words in this passage. Step Three calls for repentance, a change of direction. We must surrender our will and our lives to the care of God. The egocentric, self-serving lifestyle of addiction must be abandoned. No longer must our lives be spent in the service of our own egos, but rather in service to God and others. The egocentric, omnipotent human nature described by Dr. Tiebout as "his majesty the baby" must be dethroned.

SURRENDER—A CHANGE OF COMMAND

The repentance or turning around called for in Step Three involves not only a change of direction but also a *change of command.* It is during Step Three that we "let go and let God."

The third step involves letting go as opposed to taking control; it involves giving up as opposed to persistently attempting to manage our own affairs. We addicts are like shipwrecked sailors trying to row a leaky lifeboat in heavy seas. For our own well-being, we must abandon our boat and get into God's boat. We must allow God to stand at the helm in our lives; he must become the captain of our fate. Only then is recovery possible.

Step Three has been accurately called the "step of surrender"; in this step we surrender our will and our lives to the care of God. No longer may self—his majesty the baby—reign supreme. Self must abdicate its tyrannical throne and God must be enthroned as ruler of the recovering Christian's life. Recall the wise words offered in *The Big Book of Alcoholics Anonymous*: "Relieve me of the bondage of self, that I may better do Thy will."[1]

In effect, we take the reins of our runaway addictive lifestyles and hand them to God. We say, "Take over, God; I can't do it anymore." In so doing, we have *acted* on our faith. We have demonstrated that we so believe that God can restore us to sanity that we actually accept his charge of our will and our lives.

CONVERSION, SURRENDER, AND THE NEW BIRTH

In his work with alcoholics, Dr. Tiebout identified two internal "realities" that had been changed in his patients who had surrendered. One was the feeling of omnipotence and the other was the egocentricity characteristic of human nature.[2] He learned from observing his patients that surrender involved letting go of 1) the sense of omnipotence, 2) the inability to tolerate frustration ("I want what I want when I want it"), and 3) the expectation of immediate satisfaction of needs and wants ("I want it now!").

> Dr. Tiebout believed that what had been profoundly changed in what [one of his patients] called *surrender* was that inner sense of omnipotence, that omnipotent ego. [The patient] accepted the reality of powerlessness and human limitation . . . her delusion of omnipotence was shattered. Its dominating strength was diminished. The omnipotent ego had been dethroned.[3]

In essence, his majesty the baby—that egocentric, omnipotent human nature described by Dr. Tiebout—abdicates the throne (after a "sufficient degree" of pain and suffering) and a new ruler ascends the throne in our lives. There is a change in the *direction* of our lives (repentance) as well as a change of *command* (surrender). This is the meaning of the theological term *conversion*—we are "converted" to a new way of life with a new ruler. As Pastor John Keller states, "The mark of conversion in the Christian faith is the confession that 'Jesus is Lord.' That means that there is a new occupant on the throne."[4]

Before Jesus may be enthroned in our lives, however, the old king, his majesty the baby, must die. It is a spiritual principle that death *precedes* life. As surely as winter precedes spring, the old, sinful nature must die before we can walk in newness of life. Nature itself bears witness to this fact as a seed must be buried in the ground before new life springs from it. Jesus said, "Whoever loses his life for my sake will find it" (Matt. 10:39).

In terms of the Christian drama, the cross *precedes* the resurrection. Paul said, "I have been crucified with Christ and I no longer live" (Gal. 2:20). He was referring to his old, egocentric, omnipotent human nature that had been *put to death* at the cross of Christ. Paul wrote in another place, "For we know that our old self was crucified with [Christ] so that the body of sin might be done away with" (Rom. 6:6).

In the movie *Dances with Wolves,* the wounded Union soldier (played by Kevin Costner) mounts a horse and gallops alone toward the enemy troops. In what appears to be a suicide attempt, Costner's character repeatedly rides the length of the enemy line, allowing the Confederate soldiers to take potshots at him. Finally, in a particularly moving slow-motion scene, the hero releases the reins of his galloping horse and extends his arms wide, apparently welcoming imminent death. Leaning back in the saddle, eyes closed, arms extended wide, he resembles a man crucified on a cross. He is not killed, however, as his troops, in response to his desperate act, rally and attack.

The soldier's deed is viewed as a heroic act by his superiors and he is offered the post of his choosing. His daring act—the total surrender of his own life and symbolic crucifixion under fire—is the vehicle by which he finds a *new* life among the Plains Indians; it is also the means by which he finds himself. If a man will find his life, he must lose it first.

Jesus said, "I tell you the truth, no one can see the kingdom of God unless he is born again" (John 3:3). The spiritual rebirth described by Jesus is precisely the dethroning of the egocentric, omnipotent nature described by Dr. Tiebout, followed by the enthronement of Jesus Christ as Lord of our lives. The old selfish nature is put to death and the new man or woman in Jesus rises from the grave, born again. The new convert may justly cry out: "The king is dead; long live the King!" Thus writes Paul:

> I have been crucified with Christ and I no longer live, but Christ lives in me. The life I live in the body, I live by faith in the Son of God, who loved me and gave himself for me. (Gal. 2:20)

Paul is saying that his egocentric, omnipotent nature has died—has been put to death, crucified with Christ—and a new nature, submitted to the Lordship of Jesus, has risen to take its place.

> Therefore, if anyone is in Christ, he is a new creation; the old has gone, the new has come! (2 Cor. 5:17)

Those of us who have taken the first three steps—who 1) have admitted our powerlessness; 2) in faith have come to believe, and 3) have turned our will and our lives over to Jesus Christ—have been born again. We are new creations in Christ. As Christians in recovery from the spiritual death of addiction, we are able *experientally* to comprehend the meaning of terms that, for many Christians, remain obscure, remote, theological concepts. Let us not hesitate to share with our fellow Christians what it means at a gut level to be born again.

A Word of Caution

Pastor John Keller wisely reminds us that "in the conversion talked about by Jesus and in the letters of St. Paul, although there is something new, the old remains. Conversion does not result in the elimination of the omnipotent ego and egocentricity."[5] Although we are born again, something of the old, selfish, sinful nature remains. Like a cat with 900 lives, our former egocentric, omnipotent nature—his majesty the baby—continues to rear its ugly head, hoping to regain its old throne.

In Paul's terminology, "the old man" must be put to death *daily*. The Christian drama of crucifixion followed by resurrection is an *ongoing* one. The ancient battle between the flesh and the spirit is fought every day, one day at a time. Thus Paul writes, "I die every day" (1 Cor. 15:31). As Keller states, surrender is a process—not an event.[6]

LIVING SACRIFICES

As new creations in Christ we are to "live a new life" (Rom. 6:4). The Scripture explains how we are to walk in newness of life:

> Therefore, I urge you, brothers, in view of God's mercy, to offer your bodies as living sacrifices, holy and pleasing to God. (Rom. 12:1)

Embodied in this passage is the message of Step Three. An old hymn describes it perfectly in its title, "I Surrender All." By turning our will and our lives over to the care of God, we surrender all and become living sacrifices, dedicated to the service of the King of the Universe! We say in effect, "Everything I am, everything I have is yours, God; you take it all; I live only to serve you."

Step Three embodies the heart of the Christian lifestyle. As Chrstians, we live to serve God; we turn our will and our lives over to God. With Jesus we pray, "your will be done on earth as it is in heaven" (Matt. 6:10).

For Christians in recovery, Step Three involves a dedication of the whole person to the service of God. It is essential to recovery and the maintenance of sobriety that all of life be lived as "before the face of God." The third step must become a motto by which we live, twenty-four hours a day, seven days a week.

No Sacred-Secular Dichotomy

A point often missed by many who call themselves Christians, but one that means relapse and possible death if missed by the Christian in recovery, is this: Christianity, like the Twelve Steps, is a *way of life*! Recall that in the early days of the Church, this new religion was referred to as "the Way" (Acts 24:14). Christianity is not something we "do" on Sunday mornings while pursuing selfish interests the remainder of the week.

We must be ever mindful (mind + full) that we are not our own, that we have been bought with the blood of Jesus (*see* 1 Cor. 6:19–20), that we must present ourselves as living sacrifices to God (*see* Rom. 12:1). Whether in our interpersonal relationships with spouses, children, parents, friends, and relatives; as dedicated employees or fair-minded employers; as active participants in community life; or when all alone in our quiet times, we are on the business of the King. All that we are and do is in his service; no part of our lives is separate from our role as emissaries of the King.

Theologian and biblical scholar William Barclay writes:

> True worship is the offering to God of one's body, and all that one does every day with it . . . *Real worship is the offering of everyday life to him,* not something transacted in a Church, but something which sees the whole world as the temple of the living God.[7]

The dedication to God of all that we are and do is a hallmark of evangelical Christianity. In times past, it was mistakenly thought that only those called to the ministry were given the opportunity and privilege of serving the King with their whole lives. To the contrary, evangelical Christianity heralds the message that all of life is to be dedicated to God. Whether we make shoes or build houses; whether we sell insurance or real estate; whether we are lawyers, psychiatrists, college professors, hairdressers, dishwashers, mechanics, quarterbacks, or ballerinas—all of our lives are to be dedicated to God.

Those who attend church on Sunday morning and live like pagans the rest of the week bring insult to the name of Christ. Not without justification are these so-called Christians viewed as hypocrites by those outside the Church.

As Christians in recovery, we can ill afford to divide our lives into sacred and secular compartments. Thus, the Scripture is clear that all is to be done for God. "So whether you eat or drink or whatever you do," writes Paul, "do it all for the glory of God" (1 Cor. 10:31).

CHAPTER VIII

The Rich Young Man

STEP THREE: *Made a decision to turn our will and our lives over to the care of God* as we understood Him.

At this point, some readers may be thinking, "OK. Fine. I know I'm supposed to live a Christian life seven days a week. I understand that every aspect of my life is to be offered in service to God. So just give me the list of dos and don'ts so I'll know what to do. Tell me the rules and regulations of the game so I can play it right. Just lay it all out before me like a map so I'll know which road to follow and I'll be fine."

Well, I have good news for you, and I have bad news for you. The good news is that there is no list of dos and dont's to tell you how to live your life in service to God. The bad news is that there is no list of dos and don'ts to tell you how to live your life in service to God! As for road maps to show you the way, I can think of only one: the life of Jesus Christ. Follow him.

"But," some will argue, "I know all about churches; they're always saying 'do this' or 'do that.' Their lists are a mile long. Why, some churches have rules and regulations about everything from what you eat to what you wear! Come on, where's the list?"

Perhaps it will be helpful for us to consider a story involving a rich young man who was very good at keeping a list of dos and don'ts. The story is told in the Gospel of Matthew, chapter 19, beginning with verse 16:

> Now a man came up to Jesus and asked, "Teacher, what good thing must I do to get eternal life?"

This young man did not beat around the bush! He came up to Jesus and asked the big question straight out. And isn't that really the big question: What must I do to be saved, to get eternal life? In effect, he was saying, "Give me the list of dos and don'ts; show me the map so I can find the way."

> "Why do you ask me about what is good?" Jesus replied. "There is only One who is good. If you want to enter life, obey the commandments."
>
> "Which ones?" the man inquired. (Matt. 19:17–18)

"Which ones?" Isn't that the question asked by so many of us? "Which commandments? Which rules and regulations must I obey to inherit eternal life?" The rich young man must have been especially confused because, in the religion of his day, the Jews were required to meticulously adhere to hundreds of rules and regulations! In reply to the young man's question, Jesus said:

> "'Do not murder, do not commit adultery, do not steal, do not give false testimony, honor your father and mother,' and 'love your neighbor as yourself.'" (Matt. 19:18–19)

Notice that Jesus listed the last part of the Ten Commandments (recorded in Exodus 20). These are the specific commandments that bear on our relationship to our neighbors.

> "All these I have kept," the young man said. "What do I still lack?" (Matt. 19:20)

The rich young man was very perceptive. Intuitively he knew that even though he was very good at keeping rules and regulations, he still lacked something.

> Jesus answered, "If you want to be perfect, go, sell your possessions and give to the poor, and you will have treasure in heaven. Then come, follow me."
>
> When the young man heard this he went away sad, because he had great wealth. (Matt. 19:21–22)

Jesus did not beat around the bush either! He got right down to brass tacks and very shrewdly structured the situation to show exactly where the rich young man's heart was.

Notice that when Jesus cited certain of the Ten Commandments to the young man, he left out the first four commandments, those that bear specifically on our relationship to God (such as, "You shall have no other gods before me"). Jesus knew intuitively that, even though this young man was highly proficient at the meticulous adherence to rules and regulations, the man's heart was in his pocketbook. His wealth and riches were his god; he was a slave to his own possessions. While outwardly adhering to rules and regulations, inwardly the young man was guilty of idolatry. He put his wealth before God. He was ultimately *unwilling* to sell all he had, give it to the poor, and follow Jesus. He knew in his heart that he loved gold more than God. Thus, he walked away sad.

BEWARE THE YEAST OF THE PHARISEES

It is important to understand that though inwardly he was an idolater, outwardly the rich young man was highly proficient in meeting the external requirements of the religion of his day. From the time of the last writings of the Old Testament to the time Jesus walked the hills of Galilee, a period of about four hundred years, the religion of Judaism had undergone many changes. Judaism had become a religion of dos and don'ts, a complex system of rules and regulations. By Jesus' time on earth, hundreds of laws had been added to what had been the Judaism of the Old Testament. Rules governed nearly every conceivable facet of daily existence. There were rules for work, play, interpersonal relationships, dress, and dietary habits. The Jews had become prisoners of their own system of laws, and the Pharisees and other religious leaders were the jailers.

As an illustration of the ridiculous extremes that these laws had reached—and the clever means people used to get around them—consider the following: If a person's house caught fire on the Sabbath day, it was unlawful for him to gather his clothes and other belongings and take them from the burning structure; to do so was construed as working on the Sabbath! If, however, the person whose house was on fire put on as many of his clothes as possible and walked out of the burning house, he was not guilty of working on the Sabbath! *Wearing* all his clothes at one time was permissible; *carrying* them was breaking the Sabbath.

It was the requirements of this kind of religion that the rich young man had met. Yet, his was a religion of externals—mere superficiality—a religion that lacked depth; his was a religion that failed to change the heart.

Their insistence on the meticulous, external adherence to the letter of the law was one of the primary reasons Jesus had problems with the Pharisees and other religious leaders. When Jesus and his followers picked a few ears of corn on the Sabbath to fill their empty stomachs, they were accused of harvesting on the Sabbath and branded as lawbreakers. When Jesus healed the sick on the Sabbath, he was scorned as a lawbreaker.

Jesus had nothing good to say about those who insisted upon meticulous obedience to the letter of the law. To the crowd in Jerusalem, he exposed the Pharisees and other religious leaders for what they were:

> Woe to you, teachers of the law and Pharisees, you hypocrites! You clean the outside of the cup and dish, but inside they are full of greed and self-indulgence. . . . Woe to you, teachers of the law and Pharisees, you hypocrites! You are like whitewashed tombs, which look beautiful on the outside but on the inside are full of dead men's bones and everything unclean. In the same way, on the outside you appear to people as righteous but on the inside you are full of hypocrisy and wickedness. (Matt. 23:25–28)

Modern-Day Pharisees

Unfortunately, those who insist upon the meticulous adherence to rules and regulations did not disappear with the Pharisees of Jesus' day. Today, we all too often find an implicit *legalism* in our churches that burdens us with impossible expectations and expresses itself as a tyranny of shoulds: You should be in church every time the doors open; you should read your Bible every day; you should pray every morning—on your knees—for at least 17.6 minutes; you should teach Sunday school; you should tithe (based on pretax income, of course); you should serve on at least three committees; you should sing in the choir; you should go on mission trips; you should witness to your coworkers ("How many souls have *you* won for Christ this quarter?"); you should have quiet time every morning; you should have family quiet time twice a week; you should get along with your spouse at all times; you should set the perfect example for your children at all times; you should never complain; you should never get angry; you should never have doubts about your beliefs; you should never go to bed without brushing your teeth . . .

The result of the tyranny of shoulds imposed upon their members by too many churches is a very real sense of *guilt* felt by many Christians. This burden of guilt binds our spirits, preventing us from soaring in the freedom of Christ. The eighteenth-century English poet William Blake, himself a Christian, described the stifling oppression of institutionalized legalism:

I WENT to the Garden of Love,
And saw what I never had seen:
A Chapel was built in the midst,
Where I used to play on the green.

And the gates of this Chapel were shut,
And "Thou shalt not," writ over the door;
So I turn'd to the Garden of Love
That so many sweet flowers bore;

And I saw it was filled with graves,
And tomb-stones where flowers should be;
And Priests in black gowns, were walking their rounds,
And binding with briars my joys & desires.[1]

The institutionally sanctioned tyranny of shoulds is responsible for "binding with briars" the joy as well as the consciences and liberty of far too many Christians today. While it is one thing to be guilty as a result of the taint of original sin or to experience guilt as a result of stubborn rebellion against God's will, it is quite another thing for a Christian to be burdened with *useless* guilt because he or she fails to meet the self-righteous demands of a legalistic laundry list of dos and don'ts.

Salvation has *nothing* to do with shoulds and oughts, and the Christian life is *not* about a meticulous adherence to such lists. We *cannot* please God by keeping rules and regulations! The rich young man was good at keeping the rules, yet his *heart* was wrong. He loved money more than God.

We cannot earn our way to heaven by attending church, paying tithes, or serving on committees. This was the mistaken thinking of the Pharisees. They thought if they were "good" enough, God would reward them with salvation. They besmirched the unspeakable gift of God by thinking they could earn it.

Pastor and therapist David Seamands reminds us in his book, *Healing Grace,* that salvation is *unearnable,* that God's grace is *unrepayable.*[2] Paul said it this way:

> For it is by grace you have been saved, through faith—and this not from yourselves, it is the gift of God—not by works, so that no one can boast. (Eph. 2:8–9)

Grace is a *gift.* It is *free.* It is unmerited, unearned *pardon* from the (death) penalty of sin. Since we are saved by God's grace—his unmerited pardon—and not by deeds, actions, or works of our own, then it makes little sense to think that we must be "good" enough to "earn" our way to heaven.

God has already paid our way to heaven. The payment for our eternal life was secured by the blood of Jesus Christ. We cannot earn that which has already been freely given!

The tyranny of shoulds imposed by some churches on their members is little different from the yoke of bondage imposed upon the Jews by the Pharisees and teachers of the law. All too often we have traded one form of legalism for another. If Jesus decried the legalism of his day, he will think little more of the tyranny of shoulds imposed upon many Christians today.

THE GREATEST COMMANDMENT

Since adherence to a code of laws or obedience to a list of rules and regulations is *not* required to inherit eternal life, does this mean we can do anything we like?

When we "turn our will and our lives over to the care of God," as Step Three states, we acknowledge Jesus as *Lord* of our lives. We do not *make* Jesus Lord; he is already that. In Step Three, we *submit* to his Lordship as the ongoing process of surrender begins.

But how do we do that? Are we right back to a list of dos and don'ts? Absolutely not.

Jesus said it this way: "If you love me, you will obey what I command" (John 14:15) and "My command is this: Love each other as I have loved you" (John 15:12). Earlier in this book, we saw that "God is love" (1 John 4:16b), and his love is poured out on us in the shed blood of Jesus Christ. Since we are beings created in the "image of God" (*see* Gen. 1:26–27), it follows that we should emulate God's example by pouring out love to one another.

When Jesus was in Jerusalem during the week prior to his crucifixion, the Pharisees banded together, as they so often did, in hopes of finding a way to trick Jesus into saying something they could regard as blasphemous.

> One of them, an expert in the law, tested him [Jesus] with this question: "Teacher, which is the greatest commandment in the Law?"
>
> Jesus replied: "'Love the Lord your God with all your heart and with all your soul and with all your mind.' This is the first and greatest commandment. And the second is like it: 'Love your neighbor as yourself.' All the Law and Prophets hang on these two commandments." (Matt. 22:35–40)

For those who insist on a list of dos and don'ts, there it is! The list is short and to the point—love God and love your neighbor as yourself. All the Law and the Prophets (that is, the entire Old Testament), all the lists of dos and don'ts, all the rules and regulations, "hang on these two commandments."

The Dreadness of Freedom

To borrow the words of Francis Schaeffer, "How should we then live?"[3] The answer to the question is manifested in one word channeled in two directions: *Love* must characterize our vertical relationship with God and *love* must characterize our horizontal relationship with our neighbor. The cross, made of a vertical beam and a horizontal beam, is the supreme symbol of love.

It is as simple—and as profound—as that! God does not provide us a recipe to follow as we turn our will and our lives over to him. That's what I meant earlier when I said the bad news is that there is no script for us to follow in turning it over to God. The meticulous adherence to a script was precisely the problem of the Judaism of Jesus' day; the Jews strictly adhered to the letter of the law while ferreting out every possible loophole for "legally" getting around it. Jesus applied an Old Testament prophecy to them; he said: "'These people honor me with their lips, but their hearts are far from me. They worship me in vain; their teachings are but rules taught by men'" (Matt. 15:8–9).

Jesus was not and is not interested in legalistic dillydallying. Jesus is interested in what is in our hearts. That's why he made it short and to the point: "If you love me," he said, "you will obey what I command." He attached no list of requirements; he left no script for us to follow like actors in a play; he presented no set of instructions to obey like mindless automatons. Love God with all your heart, mind, and soul; love your neighbor as yourself. That's it! We are each personally responsible for the manner in which we serve God in accordance with these two broad guidelines.

The nineteenth-century English pastor, George MacDonald, wrote:

> The commandments can never be kept while there is a strife to keep them: the man is overwhelmed in the weight of their broken pieces. It needs a clean heart to have pure hands . . . a power of life, not of struggle; the strength of love, not the effort of duty.[4]

The rich young man who came to Jesus seeking the way to eternal life was highly proficient in his *duty;* he obeyed the commandments *outwardly.* Nevertheless, though he exerted the effort of duty, his obedience lacked the strength of love. A meticulous, dutiful, outward adherence to the Ten Commandments or any other commandments will not earn passage to heaven.

As we saw earlier, the young man's heart was wrong. God desires both the outward dedication of our bodies (*see* Rom. 12:1) and the internal dedication of our *hearts* (*see* Rom. 2:29) as living sacrifices to his will. The heart bolstered by the strength of love will go far beyond the external adherence to law all the way to the total dedication that can be motivated only by *love,* never by duty.

The main ingredient in the recipe for Christian living is love. Jesus commands us to serve him by loving one another. It is not up to the pastor, the Sunday school teacher, the AA sponsor, or anyone else to tell us how to live the Christian life of love. If we are wise, we will surely seek the counsel of other Christians in this matter, but ultimately, each of us is responsible for how we outwardly express love for God, neighbor, and self.

As mature men and women in Christ, we must blaze our own trail through the cultural wilderness and spiritual wasteland in which we live. The explorer who searches through the wilderness uses a compass to direct his way. The pilgrim who seeks the way of God also uses a compass, one whose needle always points in the direction of *love.* Go where love directs and you will blaze the right trail.

The Vine and the Branches

Since there is no list of dos and don'ts to check off, how can we know if we are growing "in the grace and knowledge of our Lord and Savior Jesus Christ" (2 Pet. 3:18)? Jesus provides an answer: He said to his disciples, "I am the vine; you are the branches. If a man remains in me and I in him, he will bear much fruit" (John 15:5).

As Christians in recovery, working a program of action, we will develop and bear fruit. The fruit will manifest itself in *changed* beliefs, attitudes, and behaviors. If we walk as Jesus walked, we will cease to live in a manner characterized by egocentricity, omnipotence, and narcissism.

Our old, addicted lifestyles were marked by the "acts of the sinful nature . . . sexual immorality, impurity and debauchery; idolatry and witchcraft; hatred, discord, jealousy, fits of rage, selfish ambition, dissensions, factions and envy; drunkenness, orgies, and the like" (Gal. 5:19–21). Sound familiar?

As Christians in recovery, we move away from these acts of the sinful nature, away from self-centeredness to Christ-centeredness. We bear "the fruit of the Spirit . . . love, joy, peace, patience, kindness, goodness, faithfulness, gentleness and self-control" (Gal. 5:22–23). As we and our loved ones see the "fruit of the Spirit" manifested in our lives, we know we have taken the path of Christian love.

SIMPLE—BUT PROFOUND CONCLUDING THOUGHTS ON STEP THREE

When we make a decision "to turn our will and our lives over to the care of God" we embrace not only the heart of the Twelve Steps but also the heart of Christian living. With this step, we acknowledge Jesus as Lord of our lives, and begin the lifelong process of surrender to God. The entire matter boils down to loving God and loving our neighbor as ourselves. Still, volumes have been written about the way of love as exemplified by the life of Jesus Christ. In searching for some way to succinctly sum up much of what has been written in this chapter, I am drawn to the simple, yet deeply profound words of Saint Augustine, one of the greatest thinkers in the history of Christian thought. His words merit serious meditation and thought over a prolonged period of time. In attempting to reach the core of Christian living in the freedom of Jesus Christ, Augustine summed it up this way: Love God—and do what you like.

CHAPTER IX

Let the Son Shine In

STEP FOUR: *Made a searching and fearless moral inventory of ourselves.*

Once we have surrendered to God by turning our will and our lives over to him, God begins within us a lifelong process of transformation. Like clay in the hands of a skillful potter, we are gradually molded and shaped by God into vessels suitable for his purposes. Theologians refer to this lifelong process of transformation as *sanctification,* the process of becoming more and more what God intends us to be. The inventory required in the fourth step can be used by God to chip away at our character defects and shape us as he would have us to be.

DENIAL

The primary difficulty in making "a searching and fearless moral inventory of ourselves" is the denial that has helped imprison us in addiction. Denial, a psychological defense mechanism that may operate consciously or unconsciously, is a refusal to see what is there. We may willingly ignore the consequences of our attitudes and behaviors, or we may subconsciously blind ourselves to reality as a means of self-protection. In either case, denial is an attempt to escape the "pain, brokenness, and human limitation" that are inherent in the human condition.[1]

Denial, the refusal to recognize reality, is also one of the reasons that the admission of powerlessness and unmanageability called for in Step One is so difficult. It is usually painful to admit powerlessness or unmanageability. Denial is a means of escaping the pain.

Denial is darkness. In denial, we are like blind people groping in the dark. Not only are we unable to see our way out of the darkness, but also we fail to recognize where we are! Jesus said, "The man who walks in the dark does not know where he is going" (John 12:35). He is speaking of spiritual darkness. In the black pit of denial, we cannot see our way. Of even graver consequence is the fact that we no longer know who we are, for people without light are unable to see their own faces.

Have you ever wondered why nightclubs or honky-tonks are dark inside? It is because sinful behavior thrives in darkness. I once visited a popular night spot on a bright Sunday morning. The smell of stale cigarette butts and spilled beer was disgusting. The dirt and stains in the carpet, invisible the night before in the dim glow of neon beer signs, were plainly visible in the clear light of day. I thought to myself, "No one would come here if they could see the dirt and filth of this place." Dirt and filth hides well at midnight. In the midnight of denial, our own dirt and filth also lie well hidden.

Jesus said:

> Light has come into the world, but men loved darkness instead of light because their deeds were evil. Everyone who does evil hates the light, and will not come into the light for fear that his deeds will be exposed. (John 3:19–20)

Persons in denial are against the light. They are like people in a dark room who rub their eyes and yell, "Turn it off!" when someone flips on the light switch. They refuse to expose their character flaws or defects to the clear light of day. They dare not engage in self-exploration for fear of what may be discovered. For these people, denial is a dark, damp dungeon; they are spiritually imprisoned by their fearful refusal to walk toward the light.

As Christians in recovery, we are called out of the spiritual darkness that is denial:

> But you are a chosen people, a royal priesthood, a holy nation, a people belonging to God, that you may declare the praises of him who called you out of darkness into his wonderful light. (1 Pet. 2:9)

THE LIGHT OF THE WORLD

While denial is darkness, God has always been in the business of turning darkness into light.

> In the beginning God created the heavens and the earth. Now the earth was formless and empty, darkness was over the surface of the deep, and the Spirit of God was hovering over the waters. And God said, "Let there be light," and there was light. God saw that the light was good, and he separated the light from the darkness. (Gen. 1:1–4)

Because darkness is contrary to the nature of our heavenly Father, he has called us, his children, out of the darkness into the warmth of his heavenly light. The fourth step provides the opportunity for us to burst forth into the light, free from the dark dungeon of denial. Jesus said:

> I am the light of the world. Whoever follows me will never walk in darkness, but will have the light of life. (John 8:12)

Light is illuminating; it brings objects into view, showing them as they are. Sunlight shining through a window illuminates the objects in a room, giving them shape, color, and texture. The beauty of a fine vase sitting on a mantel becomes apparent in the light. The rich, saturated colors of a beautiful oil painting come forth boldly as the light penetrates the room. The delicate and intricate patterns of an Oriental rug are revealed by the light as is the shape and texture of a fine piece of antique furniture standing in bold relief against the ivory light reflected from French-vanilla walls.

The same light that reveals intricate beauty, however, also exposes dirt and crud. The dust on the mantel and the cobwebs in the corner are also revealed in the illuminating light shining through the window. Hairline cracks in Sheetrock, invisible without light, become just noticeable as the sunlight filters a million particles spinning in the beam coming through the window. Thus, the light reveals both the beauty and wonder in the room as well as the dirt and crud.

SEARCHING AND FEARLESS

As Christians in recovery, we are uniquely able to make a searching and fearless moral inventory of ourselves. Because our will and our lives have been surrendered to the care of

God, we need not fear as the *light* of the *Son* searches our hearts.

Our responsibility in the fourth step is to make an inventory of all that is revealed by the "Son-light" as it shines into the depths of our being. An inventory is a list of items in stock, both the good and the bad, the usable and the unusable. Jesus, working through the Holy Spirit, provides the "searching" light that reveals both the fine and the foul in the chambers of our hearts. Our job is simply to make the list of assets and liabilities on hand as they are revealed by his light.

As Christians in recovery, we need not fear what is revealed by the searching light of Jesus Christ. *All* our sins, *all* our flaws, and *all* our shortcomings have been paid for on the cross with the blood of our Savior. In the searching and fearless moral inventory of ourselves, *nothing* will be revealed that is left unpaid for or not covered by the blood of the Lamb of God—Jesus Christ.

Take heart in the words of the Apostle Paul:

> Do you not know that the wicked will not inherit the kingdom of God? Do not be deceived: Neither the sexually immoral nor idolaters nor adulterers nor male prostitutes nor homosexual offenders nor thieves nor the greedy nor drunkards nor slanderers nor swindlers will inherit the kingdom of God. And that is what some of you were. But you were washed, you were sanctified, you were justified in the name of the Lord Jesus Christ and by the Spirit of God. (1 Cor. 6:9–11)

What a list! Go back and read it again. "That is what some of you were," says Paul. He is addressing Christians in this passage—people like you and me who have spent time in the hog pen of sin and moral depravity but since have been washed clean by the blood of Jesus. When God looks down on Christians in recovery, he does not see drunkards or the sexually immoral or prostitutes or swindlers—he sees saints.

Therefore, as Christians in recovery, our Step Four inventory need not be performed hesitantly or reluctantly. As Jesus shines his illuminating searchlight into the depths of our being, he will discover nothing not already known to him and paid for with his blood. The *purpose* of his searching light is *to reveal to us what is already known to him.* He wishes to show *us* every character defect, every flaw, every attitude, every behavior that stands in the way of the total commitment of our will and our lives to him. This is the reason Step Four must *follow* Step Three. Once we have made a decision to turn our will and our lives over to God's care, *then* he reveals to us all the hidden things that hinder our doing so. God's illuminating light is wasted on those who refuse to follow him, choosing instead to wither in spiritual darkness. The light gives life, however, to those of us who have decided to turn our will and lives over to the care of God.

> You, O Lord, keep my lamp burning;
> my God turns my darkness into light. (Ps. 18:28)

Step Four is the discovery of all the roadblocks that prevent us from freely traveling the path to recovery, the road of life. It is not a step to be feared, but one to be joyously and hopefully anticipated.

The psalmist captures beautifully the spirit of the fourth step when he writes:

> Search me, O God, and know my heart;
> test me and know my anxious thoughts.
> See if there is any offensive way in me,
> and lead me in the way everlasting. (Ps. 139:23–24)

A MORAL INVENTORY

If we rely solely on our own judgment and evaluations to make the inventory, our psychological defense mechanisms and the latent wickedness in our hearts (*see* Jer. 17:9) will cause us to "gloss over" the list. The inventory will not be deeply "searching" unless we ask Jesus himself to reveal what lies hidden in our hearts. Thus, prayer is an essential component of the Step Four inventory.

We must use God's moral law of love, as lived out in the life of Jesus Christ, as the standard against which we compare our attitudes, beliefs, and behaviors. *Webster's Ninth New Collegiate Dictionary* defines *moral* as "of or relating to principles of right and wrong in behavior." Without God's moral law of love as our guide, our understanding of right and wrong is subject to two diametrically opposite distortions: We fall either into rigid legalism on the one hand or egocentric hedonism on the other.

Our understanding of the moral nature of the inventory will be greatly enhanced if we first distinguish between *moral* and *moralistic.* When we are *moralistic,* we are judgmental and opinionated. Our language is full of *shoulds* and *oughts.* As John Keller states: "moralism is 'shouldism': You shouldn't be like that. You shouldn't do that . . . You shouldn't feel that way."[2] Moralism is about finger pointing and blaming. It is highly conditional, critical, and nonaccepting.

Moral, on the other hand, evaluates right and wrong in accordance with God's law of love, as exemplified by the life and teachings of Jesus of Nazareth. A moral inventory uses the law of love as its standard. An attitude or behavior can thus be construed as moral if its deepest motivation is love. That love may be directed toward God, toward one's neighbor, or toward oneself as is appropriate. That love is nonconditional, noncritical, and nonjudgmental; therefore, a moral inventory of ourselves is noncondemning. We evaluate the contents of our hearts in a nonjudgmental manner; we do not say, "I shouldn't be like that."

Morality (not moralism) includes "the behavior of self-acceptance, self-affirmation, and self-esteem. Morality is the behavior of God's law of love toward oneself as well as others. If we don't have that love within and toward ourself, our relationships with others are impaired!"[3] An inventory that is not moral in the sense of self-accepting and self-affirming will only produce further shame and detriment to the recovering addict's already low self-esteem. "When the shouldism goes and the person nonmoralistically can say, 'This is me and my condition, and I want to change,' the change can come."[4]

The Step Four inventory must be moral in the sense that *love* is the operative word. As the searching light of the Son reveals our character defects, sinful attitudes, selfish motives, and false beliefs, we must accept what is revealed with a nonjudgmental, nonshaming attitude. We have *already* "made a decision" to change (Step Three); the moral inventory reveals exactly what to change.

CHAPTER X

Liabilities: Pride, Greed, and Lust

STEP FOUR: *Made a searching and fearless moral inventory of ourselves.*

A useful framework for identifying our liabilities is the traditional Seven Cardinal Sins as outlined in the pamphlet on the fourth step published by Hazelden Educational Materials.[1] This framework provides a useful way to evaluate ourselves in regard to these particular attitudes and behaviors. We must fearlessly allow the searching light of the Son to show us our position relative to these sins. Then we must change our attitudes and behaviors as needed, trusting God to forgive us where we fail. The Seven Cardinal Sins are 1) pride, 2) covetousness, 3) lust, 4) envy, 5) anger, 6) gluttony, and 7) sloth.

PRIDE

Pride is "egotistical vanity—too-great admiration of one's self. Pride makes me my own law, judge of morality and my own God."[2] Pride derives directly from the egocentricity and sense of omnipotence characteristic of our old, unconverted human nature—his majesty the baby. Pride places us at the center of the universe with the implicit expectation that others exist solely for our benefit. Pride produces an overestimation of our abilities and talents, resulting in self-inflation. It is noteworthy that the Scriptures do not tell us not to think highly of ourselves; they tell us not to think *too* highly of ourselves: "Do not think of yourself more highly than you ought" (Rom. 12:3).

Pride is traditionally thought to be the sin of Lucifer, one of only three archangels created by God. Although the most beautiful of all the angels, Lucifer, the "Lightbringer," was not content with his status but desired to make himself "like the Most High." He wanted to raise his throne "above the stars of God" (*see* Isa. 14:12–14). In his arrogant pride and self-inflation, Lucifer wanted to usurp God's authority; he wanted to be God. Lucifer, the Lightbringer, was cast down from heaven by God and became Satan, the Destroyer. When we allow ourselves to become inflated with arrogant pride, we follow a dark and sinister example.

The appeal to human pride was the means by which the serpent (Lucifer/Satan) tempted Eve in the Garden of Eden. The serpent enticed the woman by telling her that eating the forbidden fruit would make her like God (*see* Gen. 3:5). In her desire to be Godlike, she (and Adam) succumbed to the serpent's lie and ate the fruit.

The desire to be Godlike is subtly manifested in the behavior identified as alcoholic grandiosity. This behavior manifests itself in the narcissism, boastfulness, and arrogance so common in alcoholism and other chemical dependencies. (I once heard a cocaine addict say that snorting that white powder made him "feel like God!") The grandiosity of addiction is equivalent to *infantile* grandiosity wherein self is conceived as the center of the universe; all others revolve around self, mere extras in the unfolding drama of egocentric grandiosity. Surrender to God, of course, is made more difficult by this pervasive character defect.

As recovering Christians, we must forsake all delusions of Godlike grandeur. We must forfeit the right to autonomous rule. The know-it-all attitude of addiction must be surrendered to an attitude of humility, accountability, and willingness.

Humility is the opposite of pride. Whereas pride works out in an arrogant, boastful, "I'm better than you" attitude, humility manifests itself in the attitude of a servant. Paul wrote:

> Do nothing out of selfish ambition or vain conceit, but in humility consider others better than yourselves. Each of you should look not only to your own interests, but also to the interests of others. Your attitude should be the same as that of Jesus Christ: Who . . . made himself nothing, taking the very nature of a servant . . . he humbled himself and became obedient to death—even death on a cross. (Phil. 2:3–8)

It is in the attitude of humility that the paradoxical nature of the Kingdom of God is clearly apparent. Jesus said, "whoever wants to become great among you must be your servant, and whoever wants to be first must be slave to all" (Mark 10:43–44).

However, beware those who take pride in their humility; they are fond of telling all that they are "nothing but a worthless wretch saved by the blood of the Lamb." Genuinely humble people do not see themselves as worthless; instead, they value themselves as beings created in the image of God. Yet, they do not overvalue themselves to the exclusion or detriment of others.

Conceit is a form of pride. Conceited people have an excessively high opinion of themselves. They love to be the center of attention. Conceit was one of the many sins of the very "religious" Pharisees. They loved publicity and the admiration of men more than they loved God. Jesus said about them:

> "Everything they do is done for men to see . . . they love the place of honor at banquets and the most important seats in the synagogues; they love to be greeted in the marketplaces and to have men call them 'Rabbi.'" (Matt. 23:5–7)

The desire for public acclaim and the accolades of others is apparent today, as well. Conceit is manifested in the types of cars people drive, in the designer clothes they wear, or in their insistence on living in the "right" neighborhood. Blatant pride leers from behind the wheel of a Porsche and thinks, "I am better than you because I drive an expensive car." While there is nothing wrong in driving a luxury car, it is sinful to derive one's sense of self-worth from it! Egotistical pride says, "I am better than you because I wear only the latest designer fashions." I once had the unenjoyable task of counseling a woman who was fond of saying, "I don't shop at Kmart; I shop only at Neiman-Marcus." Her arrogant pride was a major obstacle in the road of recovery from her multiple chemical dependencies. Of course, it is this type of pride and conceit that insists in living in Beverly Hills because "only the best people live there."

Pride, arrogance, conceit—these sins must be cleansed from the hearts of those of us in recovery. The desire for fame and public acclaim, so important to the Pharisees as well as in our culture, is opposite to the teachings of our Lord. He said, "The greatest among you will be your servant. For whoever exalts himself will be humbled, and whoever humbles himself will be exalted" (Matt. 23:11–12).

Hypocrisy is another form of pride. Hypocrisy is pretending to be something other than what one is. Jesus frequently called the self-righteous Pharisees hypocrites. He said they were "like whitewashed tombs, which look beautiful on the outside but on the inside are full of dead men's bones and everything unclean" (Matt. 23:27). Such is the essence of hypocrisy—to appear one way, yet to be another.

Hypocrisy is a natural part of prolonged addiction. From the earliest stages in the progression of our disease we pretended that it wasn't as bad as it was. We covered up and made alibis so that things would not appear as they really were. We wore smiley-faced masks to hide the emotional maelstrom tearing us apart inside. A big part of recovery, and of Christian growth, is to become real, to drop our masks and be who we really are.

In making the Step Four inventory, thoroughly root out all manifestations of pride as they are revealed to you by the searching light of Jesus. Get rid of all evidences of arrogance, conceit, hypocrisy, and boasting. Take on the attitude of a servant.

> A man's pride brings him low, but a man of lowly spirit gains honor. (Prov. 29:23)

COVETOUSNESS OR AVARICE

> Whoever trusts in his riches will fall, but the righteous will thrive like a green leaf. (Prov. 11:28)

We come now to the sin of covetousness or avarice, that is, greed. *Webster's Ninth New Collegiate Dictionary* defines avarice as an "excessive or insatiable desire for wealth or gain." Excessive and insatiable desire is part and parcel of addiction; for the practicing addict, enough is never enough. The nature of addiction precludes moderation. Moderation and addiction are as antithetical as oil and water—they do not mix! Addiction is an insatiable monster, always craving more.

The desire for more (and more) does not disappear with our first Twelve-Step meeting or with twenty-four hours of abstinence. The desire for more of everything is deeply ingrained in addiction. An insatiable desire for addictive chemicals or for the high that accompanies compulsive behaviors is easily transformed into an insatiable desire for material goods. More than a cursory examination is needed to uncover all those areas in our lives where greed is at work.

Jesus said, "Watch out! Be on your guard against all kinds of greed; a man's life does not consist in the abundance of his possessions" (Luke 12:15). Yet we live in a materialistic society, one that craves all manner of material possessions and the status and well-being that are believed to accompany them. We are bombarded with television, radio, magazine, and billboard advertisements proclaiming the false gospel of materialism: "With the purchase of this shiny new sports car you'll be the envy of everyone at the office!" "All your friends will respect you if you wear this designer label!" "Sex and romance will be yours the moment you splash on our new aftershave!" The endless parade of commercials is specifically designed to make us discontented with what we have and to desire what we do not have. "After all," they proclaim, "you only go around once, so go for the gusto!" The rampant materialism that plagues our western culture is no more clearly evident than on the bumper sticker that reads: "He who dies with the most toys wins!" The insidious lie that happiness can be purchased at the nearest sales counter is embodied in such materialistic attitudes.

Because our discontent is constantly stirred by the advertising media, we succumb to thinking that "If only I had ______, then I would be happy." Such carrot-on-a-string thinking is a misconception that prevents our being content with what we already have and keeps us performing like rats on a treadmill for material goodies that never satisfy us.

Our obsession with materialism is expedited by the false "scientific" notion that physical reality is all that exists. The existence of the spiritual realm is ignored by many of the so-called enlightened thinkers hiding behind ivy-covered university walls. They mistakenly view reliance upon a spiritual reality (God) as a regression to infantile dependence. The drive to amass worldly goods is a direct outgrowth of this misinformed half-view of reality.

Greedy materialism is an inroad to the wasteland: The more energy invested in the satisfaction of physical or sensual appetites, the less energy available to fill the soul-hollow emptiness characteristic of the inhabitants of the wasteland. The endless pursuit of material gain ultimately ends in disappointment, discontent, and despair. Remember Solomon, whom we referred to during our discussion of Step One. Though Solomon was the richest man in the world and had his daily fill of every kind of physical and sensual pleasure, he could only describe life as "meaningless, utterly meaningless!"

The recovering addict can ill afford to be party to our culture's idolatrous worship of the material. The hollowness of the addict's soul cannot be filled with shiny cars, designer clothes, or five-bedroom houses. The pursuit of the material is another form of soul poison for those accustomed to medicating their pain with chemicals or compulsive behaviors.

Do not wear yourself out to get rich;
  have the wisdom to show restraint.
Cast but a glance at riches, and they are gone,

> for they will surely sprout wings
> and fly off to the sky like an eagle. (Prov. 23:4–5)

The Christian in recovery must not be stirred to greed or covetousness by the shallow veneer of materialism brushed across our television screens by Madison Avenue professionals. As Christians, we are called upon to forsake the covetous materialism of our society. "It is imperative on us to get rid of the tyranny of things."[3] Jesus said:

> Do not store up for yourselves treasures on earth, where moth and rust destroy, and where thieves break in and steal. But store up for yourselves treasures in heaven, where moth and rust do not destroy, and where thieves do not break in and steal. For where your treasure is, there your heart will be also. (Matt. 6:19–21)

Commenting on this passage, Pastor George MacDonald wrote: "What is with the treasure must fare as the treasure . . . The heart which haunts the treasure house where the moth and rust corrupt, will be exposed to the same ravages as the treasure."[4] A moth-ridden and rust-riddled heart is of little use in the Kingdom of God. If our focus is on the horizontal dimension of earthly treasure and material gain, there is no possibility for the vertical dimension of submission to God's will to occur. Step Three is impossible for the person whose heart is ravaged by moth and rust. The psalmist said, "Create in me a pure heart, O God . . ." (*see* Ps. 51:10). The heart must be purged of the impurities left by rust and moth if it is to be totally submitted to the will of God.

How we spend our money and our time is an excellent indicator of what is truly important to us. We can tell where our hearts are by looking at our checkbook and daily schedule. Thus Jesus said, "No one can serve two masters. Either he will hate the one and love the other, or he will be devoted to the one and despise the other. You cannot serve both God and Money" (Matt. 6:24).

Dr. Kenneth Gilburth told me a paraphrase of the last part of this verse: "You cannot serve both God and cash!" This was the essential problem of the rich young man discussed earlier; rather than following Jesus, "he went away sad, because he had great wealth." He loved cash more than Christ! How many Christians today fool themselves into thinking they can serve God while engaging in the feverish pursuit of material gain? You cannot serve God and money. Greed is the characteristic of the heart which loves the material more than the Divine! Thus, the Apostle Peter reminds us to be "not greedy for money, but eager to serve" (1 Pet. 5:2).

It is not wrong, however, to desire material comfort, nor is the appreciation of nice things wrong. We must look at our *priorities.* The rich young man was not sinful because he was rich; he was sinful because he was an idolator—he loved money more than God. For the Christian in recovery, all else must be relegated to second place so that God may be served wholeheartedly. Greed is idolatry. The translators of the old King James Version of the Bible did well to translate money as "filthy lucre."

On the other hand, Pastor George MacDonald issues a sobering warning to those of us who are not rich. "But it is not the rich man only who is under the dominion of things," he said, "they too are slaves who, having no money, are unhappy from the lack of it."[5] If we allow the lack of money to make us miserable, we are little different from the rich and idolatrous young man who went away sad because he had lots of money.

Will you set your heart upon money or will you set your heart on God? Will it be cash or will it be Christ? Jesus calls upon us to get our priorities straight. He told us we cannot serve both God and cash; we will love one and despise the other. Paul cautioned his young friend, Timothy:

> People who want to get rich fall into temptation and a trap and into many foolish and harmful desires that plunge men into ruin and destruction. For the love of money is a root of all kinds of evil. Some people, eager for money, have wandered from the faith and pierced themselves with many griefs. (1 Tim. 6:9–10)

While money is not the root of all evil as some wrongly suppose, the *love of money* is a root of all kinds of evil. Heed the advise given by Paul to Timothy: "Godliness with contentment is great gain. For we brought nothing into this world, and we can take nothing out of it. But if we have food and clothing, we will be content with that" (1 Tim. 6:6–8).

The bumper sticker "He who dies with the most toys wins" is a pathetic lie. A grim Spanish proverb paraphrases Paul's words to Timothy: "There are no pockets in a shroud!" You cannot take the toys with you.

As Christians in recovery, we are called upon to forfeit the selfish, greedy, hedonistic lifestyle of addiction. We must also forsake our society's obsession with toys and every form of material gain. Rather than participate in the rat race of materialism, we must place our trust in God, putting Jesus first in our lives and trusting him to supply our needs. You cannot serve both God and cash.

> Give me neither poverty nor riches,
> but give me only my daily bread.
> Otherwise, I may have too much and disown you
> and say, "Who is the Lord?"

Or I may become poor and steal,
and so dishonor the name of my God. (Prov. 30:8b–9)

Think need, not greed.

LUST

The insatiable desire for material goods is not far removed from the excessive desire for the pleasures of the flesh. Lust is "inordinate love and desires of the pleasures of the flesh."[6]

As it does materialism, so our society encourages lust, especially in men. Witness the endless parade of X- and R-rated movies with sexual themes. Advertisements routinely use bikini-clad models to sell with sex (for example, the buxom blonde in a string bikini standing beside a farm tractor). Even music videos frequently employ sexual themes and scenes to attract viewer attention. (Did Madonna make it because she has a great voice?) It is a common and accurate criticism among both Christian and non-Christian writers that ours is a sex-obsessed society.

A Step Four inventory requires a thorough examination of our attitudes regarding sex and lust. Sexual promiscuity often accompanies prolonged chemical dependence (as it does relationship addictions, especially sexual addiction). The loss of inhibition that accompanies the use of addictive chemicals facilitates the sexual acting-out so common in the addictive lifestyle. Not only have we used and abused chemicals but also we have sexually used and abused people! The self-gratification so earnestly sought in the use of alcohol and drugs easily spills over into the arena of sexual behavior. Adultery, AIDS, venereal disease, and unwanted pregnancies routinely accompany the self-centered lifestyle that is addiction.

Once again, abstinence from alcohol and drugs does not bring an easy end to the abuse of our sexuality. In fact, it is not uncommon for sexual addiction to accompany chemical dependency. Sex, with its accompanying physiological and emotional changes, can be employed to medicate the pain of loneliness and boredom just as can alcohol and other drugs. The use of sex as a mood-altering behavior can become addictive. Many recovering chemical dependents fail to realize that they continue to abuse their God-given sexuality long after the use of chemicals has stopped.

At this point in our inventory, we must consider how we have used others sexually for our own self-centered purposes. Are we involved in relationships whose primary purpose is sexual gratification? Do we view members of the opposite sex primarily as objects of sexual gratification? In our marriages, are we as concerned for the sexual well-being of our spouses as ourselves? Are we faithful to our partners or do we continue the dishonesty, deception, and lying of our addicted lifestyles by cheating or fooling around? Can we look our spouses in the eyes and assure them that we intend to remain sexually faithful to them?

We must also consider the use of pornography in any form as an abuse of our sexuality. As we will see shortly, lust is primarily a matter of the heart. To seek sexual excitement and gratification through pornographic materials is as much an abuse of sexuality as is adultery. It makes little difference whether the material is hard-core or soft-core pornography. When it is used as a means of sexual gratification, it is an abuse of sexuality.

For the Christian in recovery, there are clear biblical guidelines for sexual behavior. For example, the seventh of the Ten Commandments states: "You shall not commit adultery" (Exod. 20:14). The Scriptures make it clear that healthy sexuality is expressed in a monogamous relationship within the context of marriage. From the beginning God has said, "A man will leave his father and mother and be united to his wife, and they will become one flesh" (Gen. 2:24). To "become one flesh" is a reference to the sexual union between husband and wife. Within this context, sex is sacred and pure. It is not wrong or dirty as some Christians have mistakenly believed. As the writer of Hebrews says, "Marriage should be honored by all, and the marriage bed kept pure, for God will judge the adulterer and all the sexually immoral" (Heb. 13:4).

To abuse our sexuality by lustfully using others for sexual gratification brings dishonor to the name of Christ. Recovery calls for the reining in of rampant, illicit sexual desires. Unfortunately, there are some in recovery who fail to see that sleeping around (at an AA convention, for example) is a continuance of the dishonest and self-serving behavior that accompanied the abuse of chemicals. Real recovery requires a cessation of sexual acting-out, for the abuse of sex is not emotionally and psychologically distant from the abuse of chemicals.

The Book of Proverbs contains numerous warnings against the dangers of adultery and other wrongful abuses of sexuality:

> My son, pay attention to my wisdom,
>   listen well to my words of insight,
> that you may maintain discretion
>   and your lips may preserve knowledge.
> For the lips of an adulteress drip honey,
>   and her speech is smoother than oil;
> but in the end she is bitter as gall,
>   sharp as a double-edged sword.
> Her feet go down to death;
>   her steps lead straight to the grave (Prov. 5:1–5)

The writer continues with an exhortation to faithfulness in marriage:

Drink water from your own cistern,
running water from your own well.
Should your springs overflow in the streets,
your streams of water in the public squares?
Let them be yours alone,
never to be shared with strangers.
May your fountain be blessed,
and may you rejoice in the wife of your youth.
A loving doe, a graceful deer—
may her breasts satisfy you always,
may you ever be captivated by her love.
Why be captivated, my son, by an adulteress?
Why embrace the bosom of another man's wife?
(Prov. 5:15–20)

An honest examination of our lustful tendencies and a sincere desire to stop acting them out should characterize Christians in recovery. It is not enough to take the pharisaical attitude that thinks, "As long as I don't actually do it (or get caught), it's OK." Lust is, after all, primarily a matter of the heart. Jesus said, "You have heard that it was said, 'Do not commit adultery.' But I tell you that anyone who looks at a woman lustfully has already committed adultery with her in his heart" (Matt. 5:27–28). Here is a prime example for the need of the clear, searching light of the Son to reveal the attitudes of our hearts. God is calling us, as Christians in recovery, to far more than a mere ethic of rule keeping. God wants our hearts and minds as well as our bodies.

In a sexually obsessed society, many face real difficulty in avoiding the adultery of the heart spoken of by Jesus; yet God desires our thoughts, emotions, and actions to be in harmony with his will for us. We need the empowerment of the Holy Spirit to enable us to turn this part of our lives over to the care of God. In no other area is Satan and our sex-crazy society so actively attempting to sidetrack those who would follow the path of God. It is incumbent upon us to seek the strength and help of our heavenly Father to find the healthy, appropriate use of our sexuality in a sex-obsessed culture.

CHAPTER XI

Liabilities: Envy, Anger, Gluttony, and Sloth

STEP FOUR: *Made a searching and fearless moral inventory of ourselves.*

Envy can be described as jealousy or resentment of another's good fortune. Envious people resent the promotion of a deserving coworker. They are jealous because a neighboring couple purchases a bigger, nicer home in a better neighborhood. Envious people are not happy when a neighbor's son or daughter is accepted into a prestigious medical school. They are jealous over a friend's new car. Rather than applauding the good fortune or blessings of another, the envious are jealous, angry, and resentful because it did not happen to them.

As in the case of greed or covetousness, the mass media fosters an attitude of envy. An unending line of television commercials reminds us of all the things we don't have. From our average living rooms, viewing the lifestyles of the rich and famous with their Rolls-Royce cars and solid gold bathroom fixtures, we are once again reminded of how "unfortunate" we are. Envy is the offspring of our media-induced discontent.

The expression "green with envy" is profoundly descriptive. When a person is sick, especially nauseated, we joke that he or she is "turning green." The green associated with nausea is akin to the green of envy. Envy makes us sick; it is poison to the soul and robs us of peace and contentment. It prevents an appreciation of our own blessings because it is other-focused. Instead of an appreciative contentment with what we have, envy stirs discontent in our hearts and an aching longing in our souls.

The Scriptures succinctly but effectively delineate the effects of both contentment and envy:

> A heart at peace gives life to the body,
> but envy rots the bones. (Prov. 14:30)

The heart rests peacefully within an attitude of contentment and gratitude; thus, Twelve-Step old-timers repeatedly encourage an "attitude of gratitude." Envy, however, precludes an appreciative attitude. Envy is like radioactive poisoning that rots the bones; it not only eats us up from the inside, but also adversely affects those around us. Envy is a robber, and peace, joy, and contentment are its prey.

Envy is one of the "acts of the sinful nature" described by Paul (*see* Gal. 5:19–21). It is listed alongside hatred, jealousy, discord, and selfish ambition. These attitudes are cut from the same cloth and are characteristic of the heart focused on self rather than God. James writes:

> But if you harbor bitter envy and selfish ambition in your hearts, do not boast about it or deny the truth. Such "wisdom" does not come down from heaven but is earthly,

> unspiritual, of the devil. For where you have envy and selfish ambition, there you find disorder and every evil practice. (James 3:14–16)

A heart filled with envy is a heart filled with self. The heart filled with envy has no room for the love of God and neighbor; envy and love cannot cohabit the chambers of the heart. Love does not envy the good fortune of others but rather applauds it. In his unparalleled description of love, Paul wrote: "Love is patient, love is kind. It does not envy" (1 Cor. 13:4).

When the Scripture warns against envy, it does so for our good. All the commandments and guidelines of Scripture are there for our benefit; God does not exercise his regal authority for his sake, but for ours. God commands us to rid ourselves of envy because envy is poisonous—it rots our bones and consumes our souls. Envy prevents us from experiencing the joy and contentment that God desires for us every day of our lives.

Envy prevents us from learning the soul-quieting lesson learned in a life marked by adversity and hardship, such as that of the Apostle Paul. Paul wrote:

> I have learned to be content whatever the circumstances. I know what it is to be in need, and I know what it is to have plenty. I have learned the secret of being content in any and every situation, whether well fed or hungry, whether living in plenty or in want. I can do everything through him who gives me strength. (Phil. 4:11–13)

Some people are able to live virtually unaffected by their circumstances; Paul was one of these people. In their hearts burns a fire so hot that it consumes everything the world, the flesh, and the devil can hurl at it, anything that would disturb "the peace of God, which transcends all understanding" (Phil. 4:7). God the Holy Spirit is the fire contained in and completely filling the heart that is content whatever the circumstances. Only as we submit to the way of God (Step Three) and disavow the way of our culture can we hope to eventually house in our hearts a spiritual fire so hot that it melts rocks. Such is the stuff of spiritual giants. Via the Twelve Steps, we too can ascend to the land of giants.

ANGER

While anger is traditionally listed among the Seven Cardinal Sins, anger itself is not sinful. Anger is an emotion and, like any emotion, is neither good nor bad in and of itself. What we *do* with the emotion of anger may be good or bad. How the emotional energy of anger is used determines the relative value of both the emotion and the consequent behavior prompted by it.

Too often, Christians automatically assume that anger is bad. Yet anger can be the energy force that motivates us to protect and defend our own boundaries as well as those of loved ones. Anger may also provide the emotional energy that leads us to right injustices or come to the aid of the helpless and needy. Righteous anger can be the emotional force that causes truth to prevail over deceit, right to prevail over wrong, and justice to prevail over injustice and unfairness.

On the other hand, anger may be used to violate the boundaries of others or to create fear in the hearts of the weak and helpless. Or, anger may be used in a self-serving fashion to avenge perceived injustices or pursue selfish ends. As an emotion, anger is neither right nor wrong; how we use it, however, may be either.

The Scriptures clearly decry inappropriate anger:

> An angry man stirs up dissension,
> and a hot-tempered one commits many sins. (Prov. 29:22)

> A fool gives full vent to his anger,
> but a wise man keeps himself under control. (Prov. 29:11)

Fits of rage accomplish absolutely nothing worthwhile and cause significant harm to those unfortunate enough to experience them. Yet it is precisely the failure to express anger appropriately that often leads to rageful outbursts of uncontrollable temper. Anger held in is like a pressure cooker exposed too long to heat—the lid finally blows off in a powerful, often violent explosion.

Anger held in, however, can have a quite different effect in some people. Depression is often viewed as anger turned inward. People who are depressed may be directing anger toward themselves that should appropriately be expressed outwardly toward another person or situation. Men or women who were abused sexually and/or physically in childhood often manifest symptoms of depression; the anger that should have been directed toward the abuser is misdirected toward themselves. The result is depression and the numerous emotional and psychosomatic ailments that accompany anger held in.

Both the pressure-cooker effect that leads to outbursts of rage and the frozen rage of anger held in (depression) benefit from the healthy expression of anger. The Scriptures make it clear that anger should be appropriately expressed:

> "In your anger do not sin": Do not let the sun go down while you are still angry. (Eph. 4:26)

Notice that the Scripture does not say that anger is sinful: It says do not allow your anger to lead to sin. Anger will not simply disappear by itself; it will be expressed, if only in increased heart rate and blood pressure ("Boy, that makes my blood boil!"). The key is to express anger in a manner that is healthy but not sinful.

As practicing addicts, we often held our anger in. Many a bottle of booze has been drunk "at" someone (often a parent or spouse) with whom we were angry. Pent-up anger is characteristic of the practicing chemical dependent. Often the booze or the drug pulled the trigger that released the rageful outburst of intoxicated anger.

As Christians in recovery, we must learn to express anger appropriately. It is foolish to think that we will not (or worse, should not) be angry from time to time, even in recovery. Besides, all those things we "drank at" or "used at" do not disappear after our first Twelve-Step meeting. In fact, in the early stages of recovery, we feel even more anger because we are no longer deadening our feelings with chemicals or compulsive behaviors.

How to manage the inevitable anger becomes vitally important. Perhaps the simplest, most productive way to express anger is to actually verbalize it. Practicing chemical dependents and other addicts usually do not know how simply to say "I am angry" when the situation calls for it. For one reason, their emotions have become such a stew inside that many have trouble distinguishing basic feelings such as glad, mad, sad, and scared. They may be mad and yet think they are scared; they may be scared and think they are mad (the physiological changes in both anger and fear are practically identical, resulting in the "fight or flight" syndrome). Learning to discern and identify emotions long medicated by chemicals or compulsive behaviors takes time and practice. Thus, an appropriate expression of anger is to verbalize it. Say "I am angry about ______." The simple verbalization of anger diffuses the emotion and greatly facilitates the prevention of both the pressure-cooker effect and the depression associated with anger turned inward.

Another appropriate means of expressing anger is physical activity. Aerobic exercise (jogging, swimming, rapid walking) is a beneficial way to release pent-up anger. The old high school coach was right when he or she said, "Walk it off," to an irate athlete.

As a therapist, I frequently prescribe the tennis racket-and-pillow remedy for pent-up anger. Two minutes of working over a pillow with a tennis racket will assuage a lot of anger. A punching bag also makes an excellent outlet for anger.

Writing letters or recording your thoughts in a journal are other effective means for the healthy expression of anger. There is something therapeutic about putting feelings on paper; they are literally moved from the inside to the outside (which is the purpose of writing down the Step Four inventory, incidentally). Keeping a diary of thoughts and feelings is of great value in releasing emotions. Writing letters to significant others with whom we are angry, whether they are living or deceased, is also helpful (these letters generally are not mailed).

The idea is to express the anger in whatever way works for you and is not dishonoring to God, for anger not expressed leads to another malady that is the bane of the recovering addict—resentment.

Anger held in and allowed to seethe and stew finally ferments into resentment, a poisonous brew of thoughts and feelings for those of us in recovery. Resentment "is the displeasure aroused by a real or imagined wrong or injury, accompanied with irritation, exasperation or hate."[1] To describe resentment as displeasure is an understatement. Resentment is a gut-wrenching plague that infects our hearts and gnaws us hollow from the inside.

Resentment springs from the grandiosity and narcissism of addiction. We resent that we are not given the respect and admiration due persons of our considerable abilities and talents; we resent not being the center of attention at the office party; we resent the menial tasks assigned us by our supervisor; we resent that everyone doesn't see everything our way!

Resentment encumbers the outward expression of love that should characterize the Christian in recovery and results in internal feelings of hostility and anger toward others. We resent it when a coworker gets a raise and we don't; we resent it when our wife goes shopping with friends and leaves us home to fend for ourselves; we resent it when our husband goes hunting for the weekend, leaving us home alone; we resent it when things don't go the way *we* want them to.

Resentment is a self-focused attitude. It records, catalogs, and stores all perceived wrongs—real or imagined. Resentment is far different from love. Love "is not self-seeking, it is not easily angered, it keeps no record of wrongs" (1 Cor. 13:5). A heart filled with love has no room left for resentment.

A tried and proven method of getting rid of resentments that is frequently discussed in Twelve-Step meetings is to pray for those against whom we hold resentments. It is suggested that, in order to rid ourselves of a resentment, we must pray for that person each day for fourteen days. Though admittedly difficult, this method works! It is a direct outgrowth of Jesus' teaching to "love your enemies and pray for those who persecute you" (Matt. 5:44).

As Christians in recovery, it is paramount that we allow Jesus to uncover every place that resentments are hiding in our hearts. Once discovered, they should be written down, thus moving them from the inside to the outside. Resentments held on to and nurtured are dangerous; they are the rungs in the ladder back into the black pit of addiction. Here, perhaps as in no other area, the Christian in recovery must cry out with the psalmist, "Search me, O God, and know my heart . . . See if there is any offensive way in me" (*see* Ps. 139:23–24). Those of us in recovery cannot afford to harbor resentments.

GLUTTONY

As surely as chemical dependency often is accompanied by sexual addiction, so too addiction to alcohol and other drugs often is accompanied by—or replaced by—compulsive overeating. A half-gallon of cookies-and-cream ice cream can alter one's mood just as can a half-pint of Kentucky bourbon!

Gluttony is the "abuse of lawful pleasures God attached to eating and drinking of foods required for self-preservation."[2] Compulsive overeating is an abuse of a lawful pleasure.

Historically, overeating has not received the same bad press as has alcoholism and other addictions. Nevertheless, food can be used to medicate and, thus, escape the pain of loneliness, depression, and numerous other moods. As is the case with alcohol and drugs, food can be used to alter moods and the accompanying behaviors. Those who have escaped the ravages of chemical dependency must be alert to the dangers of compulsive overeating. If we raid the refrigerator each time we get too mad or too sad, then we have cause for concern.

The scriptural warnings against gluttony are plain:

> Do not join those who drink too much wine
>   or gorge themselves on meat,
> for drunkards and gluttons become poor,
>   and drowsiness clothes them in rags. (Prov. 23:20–21)

> When you sit to dine with a ruler,
>   note well what is before you,
>   and put a knife to your throat
>   if you are given to gluttony. (Prov. 23:1–2)

Remember that gluttony is harmful to the body. The Christian's body is a temple of the Holy Spirit and is not to be abused; rather, we are to honor God with our bodies (*see* 1 Cor. 6:19–20). Christians in recovery must take care of their bodies rather than abuse them. Yet attend a typical AA meeting and what will you see? The cigarette smoke will be so thick you can hardly breathe and nobody will be able to make the coffee fast enough! It is amazing to hear someone at an AA meeting say, "God has saved me from alcoholism," while he or she self-induces lung cancer at the rate of three packs of cigarettes a day. This same person will likely drink twenty-four cups of coffee daily. God does not save us from addiction so that we can kill ourselves anyway with nicotine and caffeine. If total recovery is to be possible, we must eventually cease or curtail the use of all addictive substances, including nicotine and caffeine.

A word of caution is needed, however. If you are new in recovery from alcoholism or drug addiction, do not take on too much at one time. Many of us who abused alcohol and other drugs smoked heavily and drank coffee by the quart. It is unwise to attempt to quit cigarettes and excess coffee while new in recovery. Wait till you have been sober for a considerable length of time before getting rid of the cigarettes and most of the coffee. In other words, slay your dragons one at a time.

SLOTH

Sloth is laziness, not wanting to exert oneself. The disinclination to exert oneself may be physical, mental, and even spiritual. Slothfulness implies a tendency to neglect one's duties and responsibilities. The slothful person is sleepy. The Scriptures provide an ominous picture of such a person:

> Go to the ant, you sluggard;
> consider its ways and be wise!
> It has no commander,
> no overseer or ruler,
> yet it stores its provisions in summer
> and gathers its food at harvest.
> How long will you lie there, you sluggard?
> When will you get up from your sleep?
> A little sleep, a little slumber,
> a little folding of the hands to rest—
> and poverty will come on you like a bandit
> and scarcity like an armed man. (Prov. 6:6–11)

It is wise to consider this passage in more than economic terms; applied to recovery itself, it becomes an even more somber warning. It is much too easy to become lazy or complacent in recovery. We start by skipping meetings or making excuses about not having time to go; we stop reading *The Big Book*; we forget about daily meditations. Even worse for Christians in recovery, we stop reading the Bible and accompanying biblical aids, complaining that it's too difficult. Such a lackadaisical attitude often fosters an unexpected relapse.

Recovery requires complete trust in God. It also requires effort on our part. This effort, however, is not to be confused with "willing" our way to sobriety. The effort spoken of here involves doing the things we need to do to maintain recovery—for example, prayer and meditation, meetings, Bible study and other appropriate readings, and staying close to others in recovery. If we become lazy and derelict in these duties, relapse is not far away. Recovery is a spiritual process. Spiritual sleepiness—"a little folding of the hands to rest"—can be deadly.

At the opposite of slothfulness or laziness is a behavioral syndrome common in recovering addicts—workaholism.

In fact, workaholism may be more characteristic of many in recovery than is slothfulness. Workaholism is a behavioral continuation of the lack of moderation commonplace in active addiction. Addicts tend to be all or nothing; we do things whole hog or not at all. We operate at two speeds only—wide open or completely shut down. Workaholism is a manifestation of one of these two extremes.

Shortly after entering a Twelve-Step program of recovery, I enrolled in a local college to begin work on a degree (psychology, of course). As is typical of a recovering chemical dependent, I often studied forty to sixty hours a week. Fifteen hours a week would have been adequate, but at that time, new in recovery, I still manifested the "whole hog or none" philosophy commonplace among addicts. I merely exchanged chemical addiction for work (or study) addiction. Such was an improvement to be sure, but it took years for me to learn moderation—and I still struggle with it!

(As an aside, it is not necessarily bad to be totally engrossed in a productive hobby or job during the first weeks of sobriety. Such behavior is useful, for a limited time, in keeping one's mind off alcohol, drugs, or other, more destructive, compulsive behaviors.)

Workaholism functions like alcoholism and other addictions in that it provides an escape from painful feelings as well as familial and social responsibilities. "I have to work" is a convenient excuse for avoiding PTA meetings or not going to the in-laws' house for dinner. Also, by remaining totally engrossed in work-related activities, one can numb the pain of low self-esteem, shame, guilt, loneliness, and the numerous other thoughts and feelings characteristic of addiction. In other words, workaholism is a means of escaping the painful confrontation with self and, therefore, retards recovery.

MODERATION

Those of us in recovery need to learn moderation, whether in terms of greed, gluttony, work habits, or sexual practices. Moderation, however, is a foreign concept for recovering addicts. How many of us gave up alcohol only to become marathon runners? How many escaped cocaine only to work 100 hours per week? How many of us quit smoking only to gain 200 pounds? The all-or-nothing syndrome associated with active addiction is all too easily transferred to other behaviors.

For far too long, we have lived life at its extremes. We have existed at either end of a behavioral continuum, at 1 or at 10. Recovery involves living in 2 through 9—not at black or white, but somewhere in between, in that vast, largely unfamiliar, and often vague world of gray.

Moderation must be learned—but not all at once! Continual awareness of and monitoring of immoderate tendencies in thinking, feeling, and doing will eventually foster a healthy lifestyle characterized by moderation in all things.

OUT OF MEN'S HEARTS

We have investigated the liabilities portion of the Step Four inventory by examining our lives in regard to the Seven Cardinal Sins. In the final analysis, however, it is the attitudes of our *hearts* that must be revealed by the searching light of the Son if our inventory is to be valid.

Jesus himself shines the light on those attitudes we seek to uncover in our inventory. He said:

> What comes out of a man is what makes him "unclean." For from within, out of men's hearts, come evil thoughts, sexual immorality, theft, murder, adultery, greed, malice, deceit,

> lewdness, envy, slander, arrogance and folly. All these evils come from inside and make a man "unclean." (Mark 7:20–23)

The world places its value on the outside: how we look, the clothes we wear, the car we drive, our position at the office. God, however, looks at what is inside us, at what is in our *hearts* (*see* 1 Sam. 16:7). It is the attitude of our hearts that gives shape and form to our words and behaviors. As you take this Step Four inventory, pray to God that he reveal to you the attitudes of your heart. Ask him to help you change all those attitudes and personality defects that stand in the way of your serving him with your whole heart.

CHAPTER XII

Assets: A New Creation

STEP FOUR: *Made a searching and fearless moral inventory of ourselves.*

In making a Step Four inventory, it is important to identify assets as well as liabilities. Unfortunately, a sense of low self-esteem and shame underlies all forms of addiction. At a deep level, therefore, it may be very difficult for many recovering addicts to inventory their assets or good characteristics and qualities. The gut feeling "I'm not good enough" is pervasive in addiction.

The Step Four inventory, however, calls for the identification of assets as well as liabilities (the Hazelden booklet described earlier is an excellent aid for identifying assets). Therefore, I now wish to explore areas (assets) not typically discussed in Twelve-Step literature.

A NEW CREATION

Those of us who are Christians in recovery must remember that we are *new* creations. Paul wrote, "Therefore, if anyone is in Christ, he is a new creation; the old has gone, the new has come! All this is from God, who reconciled us to himself through Christ" (2 Cor. 5:17–18a).

"The old has gone, the new has come!" The old egocentric, hedonistic, self-serving lifestyle of addiction has been forgotten by God. To paraphrase the Scripture, our sins and lawless acts he remembers no more (*see* Heb. 10:17). They are cast into what someone has called "the sea of his forgetfulness."

Read again the words of the Apostle Paul cited earlier but definitely worth rereading:

> Do you not know that the wicked will not inherit the kingdom of God? Do not be deceived: Neither the sexually immoral nor idolaters nor adulterers nor male prostitutes nor homosexual offenders nor thieves nor the greedy nor drunkards nor slanderers nor swindlers will inherit the kingdom of God. And that is what some of you were. But you were washed, you were sanctified, you were justified in the name of the Lord Jesus Christ and by the Spirit of God. (1 Cor. 6:9–11)

The Church of God at Corinth, to whom is addressed the letter from which this passage comes, was composed of just about every kind of "sinner" you could name. Yet Paul does not say that is what they are—he says that is what they *were*! Their status has been *changed,* not by any good deeds or works they have done, but by the washing, sanctifying, and justifying of the blood of Jesus Christ. No longer are they considered wicked and ineligible to inherit the kingdom of God; rather, they have been placed into a *new,* saved relationship with the Lord.

Still, some readers may think, "Yes, but you just don't know how bad I am. God could never forget all the things I've done, much less forgive them!" When we think in this way, we are allowing that old, egocentric, omnipotent nature to raise its ugly head again. To think that we are so bad that even the blood of Jesus Christ cannot wash us clean is to place self once more at the center of the universe. It is saying, in effect, "I am different; I am unique; I am the worst of the worst; even God himself must make an exception of me." We must abandon that egocentricity and realize that the blood of Jesus Christ is sufficient to wash away the sins of the whole world—including ours!

IN THE IMAGE OF GOD

The chief source of our self-esteem and the foundation upon which our inherent worth is built is the fact that we are creatures created in the image of God:

> Then God said, "Let us make man in our image, in our likeness, and let them rule over the fish of the sea and the birds of the air, over the livestock, over all the earth, and over all the creatures that move along the ground." So God created man in his own image, in the image of God he created him; male and female he created them. (Gen. 1:26–27)

Theologians have haggled for centuries over the precise meaning of this passage. One thing, however, is certain about it—there is something Godlike in you and in me! In some mysterious way, we are partakers of the divine nature (*see* 2 Pet. 1:4). As beings created in the image of God, we are set apart from and are *qualitatively different* from all other living creatures.

God has called us to be rulers over his creation. The psalmist wrote:

> When I consider your heavens,
>   the work of your fingers,

the moon and the stars,
  which you have set in place,
what is man that you are mindful of him,
  the son of man that you care for him?
You made him a little lower than the heavenly beings
  and crowned him with glory and honor.
You made him ruler over the works of your hands;
  you put everything under his feet:
all flocks and herds,
  and the beasts of the field,
the birds of the air,
  and the fish of the sea,
and all that swim the paths of the seas. (Ps. 8:3–8)

Put yourself in the place of the psalmist (David). He goes out on a clear, cold night and beholds the countless stars scattered across the heavens, innumerable like the grains of sand at the seashore. In the midst of his wondering amazement, a thought occurs to him: "Wow! What must mankind be if you who made all this are mindful of us! We humans must really be something if you have made us the pinnacle of all this wonderful creation!"

Yes, we humans really are something special to God—and that includes both you and me. We are so special, in fact, that even the hairs on our heads are numbered (*see* Matt. 10:30).

ROYAL AND RIGHTEOUS

As Christians in recovery, we should also be aware that we are part of a special community and are counted among the people chosen by God. Addressing Christians, Peter wrote, "You are a chosen people, a royal priesthood, a holy nation, a people belonging to God" (1 Pet. 2:9a).

Some may still be thinking, however, that they do not deserve membership in that special community. Such is a continuation of the destructive thinking that breeds addiction—"I'm not good enough; I don't deserve to be loved!" Such thinking is not only a manifestation of the old egocentric nature, but it is also the flip side of salvation by works. In other words, if I am unloveable because of my failures and shortcomings, then it follows that my successes and achievements make me loveable. That is like saying, "My good deeds or works will make me loveable in the eyes of God and he will reward me with salvation." *Wrong!* Salvation has absolutely nothing to do with goodness, success, or achievements. By the same token, salvation has nothing to do with shortcomings and failures. Our salvation is not contingent upon our goodness or our badness. Our salvation is contingent *only* upon the finished work of Jesus Christ on the cross at Calvary.

God did not wait for us to be "good enough" before sending his Son to die for us; God himself made the first move. He bridged the great gulf that once separated us from him. Paul wrote, "But God demonstrates his own love for us in this: While we were still sinners, Christ died for us" (Rom. 5:8). God so loves you and me that he took the initiative in reconciling us to him. His loving action did not depend on our being good. He bridged the gap between us and him by sending his Son Jesus Christ to bear the penalty for our sins:

> God made him who had no sin [Jesus] to be sin for us, so that in him we might become the righteousness of God. (2 Cor. 5:21)

Commenting upon this passage, Dr. Robert McGee writes: "By imputing righteousness to us, God attributes Christ's worth to us. The moment we accept Christ, God no longer sees us as condemned sinners. Instead, we are forgiven, we receive Christ's righteousness, and God sees us as creatures who are fully pleasing to him."[1] Christians in recovery may count among their assets "the righteousness of God." The righteousness of Jesus Christ has been attributed to us. When God looks down upon *us,* he does not see failures or undeserving sinful wretches; he sees us clothed in the *righteousness* of Jesus Christ. That makes *us* of infinite value to him.

HOLY, BLAMELESS, UNIQUE

Also counted among our assets are the attributes of holiness and blamelessness (free from accusation). Paul puts it this way:

> Once you were alienated from God and were enemies in your minds because of your evil behavior. But now he has reconciled you by Christ's physical body through death to present you holy in his sight, without blemish and free from accusation. (Col. 1:21–22)

Because "Christ's physical body" was sacrificed on our behalf, we can count ourselves as holy and blameless before God.

CHILD OF GOD

Now recall the passage from 1 John quoted earlier in this book:

> How great is the love the Father has lavished on us, that we should be called children of God! And that is what we are! (1 John 3:1)

Perhaps our greatest asset is the appellation "child of God." As such, we truly stand, with our elder brother, Jesus Christ, at the pinnacle of creation!

Some of us, however, may still be harboring that nagging doubt, that lingering voice of egocentricity that says, "The idea of God's love is great, but it just doesn't apply to me, personally; it just applies to the Church as a whole. God doesn't really relate to me one on one." If this doubt still haunts you, it's time you realized something about God, yourself, and his love for you as his holy, blameless child. Allow me to explain by way of analogy.

Imagine yourself walking in the sunlight on a comfortable spring day. You stop for a moment and glance upward to feel the glow of sunlight on your face and its warmth upon your skin. As you stand there, basking in the light of the sun, someone else comes and stands beside you. He too begins to enjoy the warmth of the sunlight on his skin. That person standing alongside you in no way diminishes the sun's warmth upon your skin. Soon, a dozen people are standing there enjoying the sunlight as it warms their faces also; then, a hundred people stand beside you. But still, the presence of these other people does not diminish the amount of sunlight and warmth upon your face. You continue to feel *all* the sun's light and warmth upon your skin. As is the sun's light, so is the Son's love! You receive *all* the love of the Son. All the love of God belongs to you *personally* and is in no way diminished by the presence of other Christians. Herein is the uniquely Christian idea of a *personal relationship* with God. For God so loved *you* that he gave his one and only Son.

SPIRITUAL GIFTS

Not only does each one have a special relationship with God, but each of us has our own special characteristics and abilities. Each Christian is equipped with unique talents and skills—"spiritual gifts"—to be used in the service of the Lord Jesus Christ. Paul writes:

> Do not think of yourself more highly than you ought, but rather think of yourself with sober judgment, in accordance with the measure of faith God has given you. Just as each of us has one body with many members, and these members do not all have the same function, so in Christ we who are many form one body, and each member belongs to all the others. We have different gifts, according to the grace given us. (Rom. 12:3b–6a)

Paul compares the Church to a human body. "Each part of the body carries out its own particular function, however prominent or however humbly unseen that function may be."[2] Just as the health and well-being of the entire human body depends on the proper functioning of all its parts, so, too, does the entire Church depend on the varied contributions of its members for its overall functioning.

Theologian William Barclay states that there are some "very important rules" underlying the passage of Scripture just quoted. One is that the passage encourages us to know ourselves: "An honest assessment of our own capabilities, without conceit and without false modesty, is one of the first essentials of a useful life."[3]

One of the joys of recovery is the continual *discovery* of abilities that we did not know we had. Addiction stunted our growth. In our rigidity, we were afraid to try new things. As a result, latent talents and abilities were not allowed to surface. In recovery, as we seek to develop new ways of relating and behaving, we discover many of the talents that lay dormant in the old, addictive lifestyle. Recovery is a process of discovery, of getting to know ourselves, our limitations, as well as our abilities and talents. It is not unusual to hear a recovering person say with surprise after some new accomplishment, "I never knew I could do that!" As Christians in recovery, we may discover talents for use in the service of God and his people that we never knew we had.

Another important rule underlying this passage of Scripture is that "it urges us to accept ourselves and to use the gift God has given us. We are not to envy someone else's gift and regret that some other gift has not been given to us. We are to accept ourselves as we are, and use the gift we have. The result may be that we have to accept the fact that service for us means some humble sphere and some almost unseen part."[4] We cannot all be pastors or ministers of music; the Church could not function if we were. The body of Christ, the Church, has *many* parts and each is essential for the overall functioning and well-being of the body. Paul writes in another place:

> Now the body is not made up of one part but of many. If the foot should say, "Because I am not a hand, I do not belong to the body," it would not for that reason cease to be part of the body. And if the ear should say, "Because I am not an eye, I do not belong to the body," it would not for that reason cease to be part of the body. If the whole body were an eye, where would the sense of hearing be? If the whole body were an ear, where would the sense of smell be? But in fact God has arranged the parts in the body, every one of them, just as he wanted them to be. If they were all one part, where would the body be? As it is, there are many parts, but one body. (1 Cor. 12:14–19)

Without a diversity of parts and functions, the body of Christ, the Church, cannot survive. Some will be teachers; others will visit the sick. One will drive the church bus, and another will repair the peeling paint in the sanctuary. Some will work in the nursery while others take food to shut-ins. One will chair a committee and another will take toys to needy children at Christmastime. It does not matter whether the service is performed within the walls of the church building, in an urban ghetto, or in a youth camp out in the woods, for there are innumerable responsibilities and opportunities for service in the body of Christ; *all* are essential for the body's functioning. We must honestly and accurately assess our gifts and learn to use them in the service of Jesus Christ.

William Barclay adds the interesting point that whatever gift we have comes from God. These gifts (or *charismata* in Greek) could not have been acquired on our own.[5] Some of us are highly skilled musicians; others are skilled craftsmen or teachers. Some of us are gifted in our speaking abilities while others are gifted writers. Whatever the gift, its source is God. As such, the gift is put to its proper use when used for his service. Each and every one of us, as Christians in recovery, have our own gift or gifts. It may be carpentry, gardening, farming, accounting, public service, playing a musical instrument, singing, teaching children, or playing sports. Whatever the gift, it is "something plus" given us by God. As Christians in recovery, it is proper that we discover, over time, the gift s given us by God and use them in his service.

Finally, whatever one's gift, it must be put to use, and the motive for its use must be "contribution to the common good" rather than personal gain or prestige.[6] In other words, talents long used in the service of self may now be used in the service of the King! As Paul said, "So whether you eat or drink or whatever you do, do it all for the glory of God" (1 Cor. 10:31).

GOD REDEEMS EVERYTHING

Also included in our inventory of assets must be those talents and abilities of which we have long been aware, but were used in the service of self rather than the service of God.

During the days of active addiction, our actions were usually self-serving; whatever we did was for the service of self rather than for the glory of God. It is not that our talents and abilities were not genuine; they were simply misdirected.

Consider the Apostle Paul as a case in point. Prior to his surrender to the Lord Jesus Christ, Paul was "extremely zealous" regarding the religion of Judaism. In his zeal, he "persecuted the Church of God and tried to destroy it" (*see* Gal. 1:13–14). He was a brilliant scholar, trained under the renowned teacher Gamaliel. After his conversion to Christianity, Paul's formerly misdirected zeal was now redirected to the service of Jesus Christ. His brilliant theological mind was used to write fourteen books ("epistles," or letters) of the New Testament. The skills he had misused to persecute God's Church were now used to establish churches throughout Asia Minor and Greece. When Jesus Christ bought Paul with his blood, he also bought Paul's theological mind and leadership skills. That which had formerly been misdirected was now redirected to the service of the King.

Charles Colson is another case in point. He is a highly trained lawyer with a brilliant legal mind. Prior to his conversion to Christianity, his skills had been used to climb the political ladder so high as to have an office in the White House itself. The misdirection of his abilities and talents in the legal profession landed him in prison after the Watergate scandal. While in prison, Colson surrendered to the Lord Jesus. Now his brilliant legal mind is used in the service of the King. Colson is founder and president of Prison Fellowship ministries, an organization that brings the gospel of Jesus Christ to those in prison and seeks to improve living conditions in prisons throughout the world.

Christians in recovery also possess numerous talents and abilities that were formerly misdirected but may now be redirected in the service of the King. The fast-talking used-car salesman who, without qualm, peddled lemons to unsuspecting customers might now use his "gift of gab" to raise funds for a church. The musician who once worked the bar and honky-tonk scene might now use her talent to make a valuable addition to a church's music program. The former gang member might use his street knowledge to aid a church's outreach to inner city youth. A former drug dealer and addict could use her life story as a witness and warning to the young people at a church youth camp. One whose addiction led to a painful divorce might comfort and counsel divorcees as part of her church's ministry to singles. The talents and abilities—as well as the pain—of the past can all be placed in the service of the King.

It is important to realize that God has called you to be *you.* He has redeemed not only your soul but also your unique personality, talents, and abilities. When God redeemed you with his blood, he bought you. You are the one he knew from the time you were conceived in your mother's womb. When you were spiritually born again, your old identity was not destroyed; your unique characteristics and talents were not discarded into the wastebasket; rather, your old, sinful, egocentric nature was put to death. In the realm of your existence, a new King ascended the throne; the old king, the self-centered ego, was dethroned. You became a partaker of the divine nature; the Holy Spirit of God joined with your spirit but did not replace it. You continue to be the unique person you have always been.

More accurately, you continue in the *process* of *becoming* the person God has always meant for you to become. From the moment of your conception, God, who sees the things yet to be as though they already were, could see the finished product he would have you become. Your personality, talents, and abilities are the ingredients from which God creates a unique recipe.

Yet, a mistake often made by new Christians (myself included) is to try and become "like everybody else." New Christians try to emulate the preacher or the Sunday school teacher or the seminary professor. In so doing, they lose their identity as unique creatures in Christ. They try to force themselves into molds they do not fit, copying this super-Christian or that one. In trying to be like someone else, we stop being who God made us to be. It is the well-intentioned attempt to conform that usually results in frustration and disillusionment.

It is important to realize that each of us, as Christians in recovery, is a new and unique creation in Christ. Each of us is capable of filling a place in God's heart that no other can fill.[7] God is the Master Potter and each of us is a unique lump of clay in his hands. We must allow God to mold us into the vessels he intends us to be. Only then can each of us fulfill the unique purpose he has for us.

INTO ACTION

In the Step Four inventory, we allow the searching light of Jesus to illuminate the innermost chambers of our hearts. His light reveals both the good and the bad, the assets as well as the liabilities. It is now time to use the spiritual illumination of Step Four as a motivation for action. With the next step, perhaps as never before, we begin to unload the burden of guilt that has weighted us down so long.

CHAPTER XIII

Confession

STEP FIVE: *Admitted to God, to ourselves, and to another human being the exact nature of our wrongs.*

God's law of love states that we are to love God with all our heart, mind, and soul (the first great commandment), and that we are to love our neighbor as our self (the second great commandment). All the relationships for which we have been created are encompassed in the moral law of love: There is the vertical relationship with God and the horizontal relationship with neighbor and self. All three relationships—with God, with neighbor, and with self—are involved in Step Five.

ADMITTED TO GOD

"Confession of sin *to God* is of the essence of true repentance; for a man who will not look up and acknowledge his iniquity manifestly does not clearly see or deeply feel its evil. Only through unreservedness of heart towards God can we enjoy peace with Him," writes theologian Robert

Johnstone.[1] Confessing or admitting the exact nature of our wrongs to God is an essential part of the program of recovery.

We have all heard the old adage "Confession is good for the soul." The Psalms provide a prime example of the need for confessing our sins and faults to God:

> When I kept silent,
> my bones wasted away
> through my groaning all day long.
> For day and night
> your hand was heavy upon me;
> my strength was sapped
> as in the heat of summer.
> Then I acknowledged my sin to you
> and did not cover up my iniquity.
> I said, "I will confess
> my transgressions to the Lord"—
> and you forgave
> the guilt of my sin. (Ps. 32:3–5)

Notice the terrible effect that silence had on David, the composer of this psalm: In his failure to confess or admit his faults and sins to God, his "bones wasted away through [his] groaning all day long." He literally felt rotten; he was depressed, sickened, and in despair. His "strength was sapped" such that he was physically weakened by withholding his confession of sin from God. With confession, however, came relief. The burden of guilt was removed when David admitted his sins to God. In David's case, confession was clearly "good for the soul."

Our sins create a *barrier of our own making* between ourselves and God. As we continue in our sin, God begins to feel far off. It is as if he has abandoned us; our relationship with him is strained. In reality, however, it is not God who has gone far away; like the Prodigal Son, it is we who have left the realm of the Father. Our sinful and selfish deeds have separated us from God, created a self-imposed barrier between us and him. The Scriptures bear witness to the separation between us and God that occurs as a result of our unconfessed sins:

> Surely the arm of the Lord is not too short to save,
> nor his ear too dull to hear.
> But your iniquities have separated
> you from your God;
> your sins have hidden his face from you,
> so that he will not hear. (Isa. 59:1–2)

When we acknowledge our sins and confess them to God, that wall of separation comes tumbling down; then, we are restored to a right relationship with our loving, forgiving Father. John writes:

> If we claim to be without sin, we deceive ourselves and the truth is not in us. If we confess our sins, he is faithful and just and will forgive us our sins and purify us from all unrighteousness. (1 John 1:8–9)

Notice the first part of this passage: "If we claim to be without sin, we deceive ourselves." This part of the passage is reminiscent of the denial and self-deception so prevalent in active addiction. We human beings will go to great lengths to deny or avoid responsibility for our sins, seeking to place the blame on heredity, environment, temperament, or even physical condition. We may try to blame someone else for our actions or say that they misled us. "It is characteristic of us all that we seek to shuffle out of the responsibility for sin," states William Barclay.[2]

Christians in recovery can ill afford to continue the denial and self-deception that were a trademark of the using or drinking days. The confession called for in the fifth step is the means by which that wall of denial and deception may finally be broken down so that it no longer acts as a barrier to the truth.

When we sin, "defenses and excuses and self-justifications are completely irrelevant. The only thing which will meet the situation is humble and penitent confession to God, and, if need be, to men."[3] Humble, penitent confession is of great value to God. The Apostle John writes in this passage that "if we confess our sins he is faithful and just and will forgive us our sins." "Scripture is full of the promise of mercy to the (person) who comes to God with the broken, the contrite, and the penitent heart. God has promised that he will never despise the penitent heart; God will not break his word; and if we humbly and sorrowfully confess our sins, God will forgive."[4]

King David of Israel was a man with the same human weaknesses as the rest of us: His lust for Bathsheba led to his adultery with her, and he even sent her husband away to be killed. Finally, David was compelled to face up to his sin when he was confronted by the prophet Nathan. In his deep sorrow and repentance, David composed the memorable Fifty-first Psalm, "one of the greatest confessionals that has ever been written."[5] This passage of Scripture shows us that, even in the face of great sin, God will hear our prayers of confession and penitence. David wrote:

> Have mercy on me, O God,
> according to your unfailing love;
> according to your great compassion
> blot out my transgressions.
> Wash away all my iniquity

and cleanse me from sin.
For I know my transgressions,
and my sin is always before me.
Against you, you only, have I sinned
and done what is evil in your sight,
so that you are proved right when you speak
and justified when you judge.
Surely I was sinful at birth,
sinful from the time my mother conceived me.
Surely you desire truth in the inner parts;
you teach me wisdom in the inmost place.
Cleanse me with hyssop, and I will be clean;
wash me, and I will be whiter than snow.
Let me hear joy and gladness;
let the bones you have crushed rejoice.
Hide your face from my sins
and blot out all my iniquity.
Create in me a pure heart, O God,
and renew a steadfast spirit within me.
Do not cast me from your presence
or take your Holy Spirit from me.
Restore to me the joy of your salvation
and grant me a willing spirit, to sustain me.
Then I will teach transgressors your ways,
and sinners will turn back to you.
Save me from bloodguilt, O God,
the God who saves me,
and my tongue will sing of your righteousness.
O Lord, open my lips,
and my mouth will declare your praise.
You do not delight in sacrifice, or I would bring it;
you do not take pleasure in burnt offerings.
The sacrifices of God are a broken spirit;
a broken and contrite heart,
O God, you will not despise. (Ps. 51:1–17)

In this unforgettable psalm of confession, David did not make excuses for his sins; he *confessed* them and sought forgiveness. Denial, rationalization, minimizing, blaming, and the numerous other defenses we use to avoid responsibility for our sins hinder us from seeking and, thus, receiving the forgiveness of our heavenly Father. Making excuses for our sins, faults, and shortcomings (seeking self-justification) only hardens our hearts and prevents us from penitently seeking the forgiveness of our loving Father. "The very fact of humble confession opens the door to forgiveness, for the man with the penitent heart can claim the promises of God."[6]

The prayer of confession is like the sweet aroma of incense rising heavenward to please God. His promises make it clear that he is pleased when his child in recovery takes the fifth step. Thus, "the essence of the Christian life is, first, to realize our sin; and then to go to God for that forgiveness which can wipe out the past, and for that cleansing which can make the future new."[7]

> He who conceals his sins does not prosper,
> but whoever confesses and renounces them finds mercy. (Prov. 28:13)

ADMITTED TO ANOTHER HUMAN BEING

The practice of confessing or admitting one's sins to another person is an ancient practice. It is seen in the ministry of John the Baptist: "People went out to him from Jerusalem and all Judea and the whole region of the Jordan. Confessing their sins, they were baptized by him in the Jordan River" (*see* Matt. 3:5–6). John Wesley, the founder of Methodism, taught the practice to his followers. They met two or three times a week to confess their sins to one another.[8] The basis for the practice is the following passage from the Book of James:

> Therefore confess your sins to each other and pray for each other so that you may be healed. (James 5:16a)

Confession to God as well as to another human being goes hand in hand. William Barclay writes, "To be effective, confession of sin has to be made to men, and especially to the person wronged, as well as to God. In a very real sense it is easier to confess sins to God than it is to confess them to men; and yet in sin there are two barriers to be removed—the barrier which sin sets up between us and God, and the barrier which sin sets up between us and our fellow-men. And if both these barriers are to be removed, then both kinds of confession must be made."[9]

It is an inherently healing act to unload, in the presence of another human being, the burden of guilt that has been part and parcel of the lifestyle of addiction. "Many people who have participated in the Fifth Step speak of their experience in these terms: relief from a heavy weight or sack, and a sense of being cleansed." [10]

Dr. Kenneth Gilburth has said that, in the spiritual realm, to *admit* something is to get rid of it. Such is a manifestation of the paradoxical idea that to save one's life, one must lose it. Dr. Edward Sellner writes, "In some mysterious way, it is only by speaking out, verbally acknowledging our mistakes, failures, and anxieties to another person that the power of those feelings and deeds lose their control over us."[11]

In the deeply intimate fifth step, the loneliness and isolation of the addictive lifestyle may be remedied. Thoroughly done, there will be a level of openness and honesty never before experienced. The intimacy, openness, and honesty of this step will create a connectedness with another human being that may mark our reentry into the sphere of healthy human relationships. It is as if we have at once rejoined the world of healthy, functioning men and women as our burden of guilt is lightened in confession. The intellectual belief in the forgiveness of sin may be *experienced* (felt)—perhaps for the first time—at a deep level as we undertake the act of intimacy and humanness that is the fifth step.

ADMITTED TO OURSELVES

In the fourth step, we made a searching and fearless moral inventory of ourselves. In that step of discovery, we cataloged our assets and liabilities. In the fifth step, we go beyond the inventorying of character defects, faults, and shortcomings; in this step, we *own* them. That which is discovered in the fourth step is claimed in the fifth step. It is not enough to simply ascertain our weaknesses and limitations. We must go beyond cataloging; we must *accept* what is found.

Once again, the wisdom of the Twelve Steps is apparent as Step Five asks us to admit to *ourselves* the exact nature of our wrongs. We can admit to another human being an endless list of character defects and shortcomings without ever believing they truly apply to us; we can fool ourselves into believing that beneath a comparatively shallow layer of common human limitations there is an exceptional human being, different than and superior to others. We can even confess to God a list of sins and still utterly fail to realize the nature of our sinful condition. But if we are to complete the fifth step, we cannot get away with lying to ourselves. We must not only admit but also *accept* the exact nature of our wrongs. We must see ourselves as sinful human beings who are utterly incapable of earning salvation or meriting the bountiful grace of God. We must lower our masks, look into the mirror and accept ourselves as persons who are limited and flawed, yet deeply loved by God. Perhaps as at no other place in the steps of recovery, the fifth step compels us to be rigorously honest with *ourselves.* Pastor John Keller writes:

> Confession is unfulfilled unless there is the desire and willingness to change. Changes in attitudes, feelings, and behavior will come only when there is acceptance of what needs to be changed. Acceptance deep within oneself is essential for change, and that acceptance is part of true confession.[12]

King David, the writer of many of the Psalms, was compelled to face himself and accept the grievous nature of his sins. He had committed adultery with Bathsheba and had sent her husband away to be killed. He came to his senses after being confronted by Nathan the prophet and was deeply sorry for his sinful acts. He not only confessed his sin to God, but he also admitted to himself the exact nature of his wrongs. He wrote:

> For I know my transgressions,
> and my sin is always before me.
> Against you [God], you only, have I sinned
> and done what is evil in your sight,
> so that you are proved right when you speak
> and justified when you judge. (Ps. 51:3–4)

Not only did David acknowledge his transgressions but he was also aware of and acknowledged his sinful condition as a human being born into a fallen world. He wrote, "Surely I was sinful at birth, sinful from the time my mother conceived me" (Ps. 51:5). His acceptance of his sinful condition brought with it a desire to change his attitudes, feelings, and behaviors. He continued, "Cleanse me with hyssop, and I will be clean; wash me, and I will be whiter than snow . . . Create in me a pure heart, O God, and renew a steadfast spirit within me" (Ps. 51:7, 10).

Our sinful condition is part of our common human inheritance, passed down from Adam and Eve. That sinful condition is precisely the egocentric, omnipotent human nature that strives to enthrone self, rather than God, as the guiding force in our lives!

In completing the fifth step, we must face our spiritual kinship with Adam and Eve in our common human desire to be god in the place of God. Our first human ancestors succumbed to the serpent's lie that they could be "like God" (*see* Gen. 3:5). As their children, we all have followed the example of our first parents. The pervasive human desire to place self above God is the essential nature of what the Bible calls "sin" and what the fifth step refers to as "the exact nature of our wrongs." Only as we honestly face our inherent human desire to dethrone God and reign in his place will we truly understand the *exact* nature of our wrongs. All our faults, flaws, character defects, and sins will ultimately be traceable to our egocentric, omnipotent, selfish desire to be god in the place of God.

The acceptance of our sinful condition, demonstrated by the honest admission to ourselves of the exact nature of our wrongs, will show us the need for the continual cleansing power of the blood of Jesus Christ and bring us to the next step in the program of recovery—readiness to have God remove all our defects of character.

CHAPTER XIV

Entirely Ready, Humbly Asked

STEP SIX: *Were entirely ready to have God remove all these defects of character.*

STEP SEVEN: *Humbly asked Him to remove our shortcomings.*

The sixth step is a continuation of the *process* of surrender that runs throughout all the steps, but is most clearly evident in Step Three. Step Six derives directly from Step Three, in which we turned our will and our lives over to the care of God. In the sixth step, our willingness to turn it all over to his care continues, and we implicitly admit that God is in charge of us now. Thus we cannot take Step Six if we have not already taken Step Three.

Surrender means we have stopped fighting; we have relinquished control of our lives to God; we no longer try to run our own show. In the framework of Step Six, surrender means that we cease trying to re-create *ourselves* in the image of God and become willing to be molded and shaped by God into fit vessels for his use.

The emphasis in Step Six is on God—not on self. We become entirely ready to have *God* remove our defects of character. In both Steps Six and Seven, "we need to remind ourselves of our powerlessness . . . We need to get out of the pattern of thinking that makes us feel that we are all-powerful, that our powers can remove these defects of character . . . Just as we are powerless over alcohol (and any number of other things), so we are powerless to remove our defects of character. We need help."[1] The task of removing all these defects of character is much too great for mere human endeavor. Once again, the wisdom of the Twelve Steps is evident in that Step Six does not suggest we remove our own defects of character; instead, it states that we were entirely ready to have *God* remove them.

There is also a direct relationship between the sixth step and the first step. Recall in our discussion of Step One that the admission of powerlessness is particularly distasteful to those of us raised in western culture. Our society teaches us—drums into our heads, in fact—that we can accomplish anything if we just put our minds to it and try hard enough. We worship the great achievers, from the seven-figured sports star to the Hollywood actress. Our parents, teachers, favorite aunts and uncles, and even politicians have all taught us to "go for it," to make it all happen ourselves. Yet this do-it-yourself attitude is not only a roadblock to the admission of powerlessness, but also is exactly contrary to the message of Step Six, in which we are entirely ready to have God do it for us. While society may sternly admonish us to "pull ourselves up by our own bootstraps," Step Six encourages us to let go and let God.

ENTIRELY READY

Not all, however, are "entirely ready" to ask God to remove their defects of character. Their unwillingness and hesitancy manifests itself in certain attitudes and behaviors.

First, some recovering addicts want to hang on to a few of their favorite character defects, those harmful or sinful behaviors that they are unwilling to give up. For example, there is the businessman who is honest in his business transactions with customers, but continues to cheat on his income tax. Or, if he doesn't cheat on his income tax, he cheats on his wife. There is the woman who gives up Valium but chooses, instead, to eat a half-gallon of ice cream each day. Then there is the aristocratic lady who is very comfortable with her pride and has no intention of letting go of that. How could she deign to be like everyone else? Also, there is the envious salesperson who continues to stew over the successes of coworkers, wishing them ill rather than well. What would she do without envy to motivate her? Finally, there is the attention-seeker who insists on being the life of every party, the star of every show. How could he possibly surrender his position as the center of attention? These lingering attitudes and behaviors are manifestations of the old egocentric, omnipotent nature—his majesty the baby. That inner, egocentric tyrant dies hard, never wanting to surrender completely. Step Six, however, like Steps One and Three before it, calls for total—not partial—surrender.

Being entirely ready to have God remove all our defects of character is a tall order. If we examine our hearts thoroughly enough, we will likely discover a few favorite flaws that we are not yet willing to surrender. Fortunately, this step, like the others, is an ongoing process. It does not have to be done perfectly—but it must be done sincerely and honestly. Remember the Twelve-Step slogan—"we seek progress, not perfection!"

Second, some in recovery want to "clean up their act" before going to God.[2] Like people who clean the house before the new maid arrives so that she will not see how they live, these people are ashamed of themselves and their lifestyles and do not want God to see them as they are. Like Adam and Eve in their newly discovered nakedness, they hide from God (*see* Gen. 3:8–10). These persons have yet to claim God's word as revealed to us through the prophet Isaiah:

> "Come now, let us reason together,"
> says the Lord.
> "Though your sins are like scarlet,
> they shall be as white as snow;
> though they are red as crimson,
> they shall be like wool." (Isa. 1:18)

These persons have failed to realize how deeply God identifies with our humanness. God understands us because he became one of us as the human being, Jesus of Nazareth. He is personally and intimately familiar with the pains and difficulties of our lives in a fallen world. Like us, he has experienced the temptation of sin. Speaking of the ascended Jesus, the writer of Hebrew reminds us that "we do not have a high priest [Jesus] who is unable to sympathize with our weaknesses, but we have one who has been tempted in every way, just as we are—yet was without sin" (Heb. 4:15). Because Jesus Christ is our loving, empathetic High Priest and Savior, it is not necessary for us to "clean house" before taking all our defects of character to God. As James Brandon suggests, we need only "present Him with the reality of ourselves, instead of our dreams and wishes of how we want to be. It is not necessary to present ourselves to God in any other way than as we actually are."[3]

Third, some in recovery *fear* going before God in the nakedness of their exposed souls. Like Step One, the sixth step is one of reality. We must be ready to go before God without pretense, leaving behind the masks worn in our social transactions. "One of the potentially frightening aspects of working Steps Six and Seven is that they require us to deal directly with God. We are left alone to communicate directly with our God; to look at our relationship with Him in the privacy and loneliness of our own hearts and minds."[4] To stand bare and naked before the Creator of the Universe is a potentially terrifying experience for many.

For the Christian in recovery, however, terror and fear may be replaced by trust and hope. Christians do not have to fear going before God, even with all their defects of character clearly exposed. The writer of Hebrews has already told us that we have a High Priest, Jesus Christ, who, after being subjected to all the kinds of temptations just as we are, ascended to the throne of God. We may, therefore, "approach the throne of grace with confidence, so that we may receive mercy and find grace to help us in our time of need" (Heb. 4:16).

The Christian in recovery need not fear Step Six. Our Savior, Jesus Christ, is in heaven acting as intermediary (High Priest) between us and the Father. None other than Jesus Christ himself pleads our case for us, day and night. No lawyer on earth is as capable and willing to speak for us as is our ascended Savior! As the writer of Hebrews put it, "he is able to save completely those who come to God through him, because he always lives to intercede for them" (Heb. 7:25).

HUMBLY ASKED

Once we are entirely ready to have God remove our defects of character, it is time to humbly ask him to do so. Before we ask God, however, we must ask ourselves if we truly believe God can remove all these defects of character. This question can be answered affirmatively only if we have already taken Step Two—"came to believe that a power greater than ourselves could restore us to sanity." If we have not taken Step Two, we cannot take Step Seven.

The restoration to sanity spoken of in Step Two requires that the sinful, egocentric human nature be subjugated to the will of God; thus, Step Two leads quite naturally to Step Three. The process of surrender that is woven throughout the steps is the process of turning over to God our wills and our lives. Surrender, then, involves the subjugation of human will to divine will.

It is important to realize, however, that the subjugation of the omnipotent, egocentric self is a *cooperative* effort between God and humans. If we successfully subjugate that nature on our own, without the help of God, a far greater danger arises as the result of that very success: the danger of hubris—inflated pride and self-satisfaction. "I did it on my own. I don't need any help, not even from God."

It is at this point that we see the intimate connection between Steps Seven, Two, and One. In the second step, we came to believe that a power greater than ourselves could restore us to sanity. In Step One, we admitted our inability (powerlessness) to subjugate various aspects of our attitudes and behaviors, especially our addictive behaviors. If at Step Seven, we cling to the lingering misconception that we are capable, by ourselves, of subjugating our omnipotent, egocentric natures, then we have not taken Steps One or Two! As both the seventh and second steps imply, "true victory over self is the victory of God in the man, not of the man alone. It is not subjugation that is enough, but subjugation by God."[5]

The seventh step, like the second, requires faith. Faith is believing that God *can* and *will* do what he says he will do. He has told us that though our sins are "like scarlet, they shall be as white as snow" (Isa. 1:18). In the inspired wisdom of the Twelve Steps is the promise that God will remove all our defects of character. Certainly our lives have repeatedly demonstrated that we cannot do this ourselves. Truly, in the seventh step, as in so many others, we must let go and let God. The process of surrender goes on.

Step Seven states that we *humbly* asked God to remove our shortcomings. In this step, we must come to God as his humble servants. We must recognize our *need,* not only for his provision in the material arenas of life, but also for healing in the spiritual, psychological, and emotional spheres of life. To continue in sobriety and recovery, we must recognize the absolute necessity of God's miraculous intervention in our lives. If God does not change us, relapse is inevitable. Thus, when we ask God to remove our shortcomings, we must swallow our pride and humbly recognize that our *lives* depend on his response to our prayer. Humility derives from the recognition of our total *dependence* on him to transform us so that continued recovery and well-being are possible.

On the other hand, our total dependence on God to change us does not mean that we are totally passive and inert. The transforming process that is the Twelve Steps is a *cooperative* effort between us and God. Where God leads, we follow. What God commands, we obey. When God says trust, we act on that trust. As we shall see, God is the Master Potter; we are to be willing, pliable clay in his hands.

The Potter and the Clay

"We must change!" is a phrase I heard over and over in my first Twelve-Step meetings. I failed to appreciate the magnitude of those words in the early days of my recovery because I failed to see the need for me to change. I thought giving up alcohol and drugs was enough. Today, I am grateful to Gary, the man who kept saying over and over, "We must change!" (It seems he was always looking at me when he said that. He probably knew I hated to hear it.) After years of recovery, I would expand his wise saying as follows: "We must allow God to change us." This is, of course, the message of Step Seven.

The seventh step entails a process of transformation wherein God is the Master Artisan and we are the vessels upon whom he works his craft. The Scripture states it thus:

> Yet, O LORD, you are our Father.
> We are the clay, you are the potter;
> we are all the work of your hand. (Isa. 64:8)

Just as the potter molds and shapes the clay into various forms depending on the intended use, so God molds and shapes us into fit vessels for his specific purposes. The clay does not choose the method by which it is shaped—such is the province of the potter. Thus, Paul emphasizes God's preeminence as Master Potter and Craftsman when he writes, "For we are God's workmanship, created in Christ Jesus to do good works, which God prepared in advance for us to do" (Eph. 2:10).

Trial by Fire

The removal of our shortcomings is less often an instantaneous and divine act than the more common "trial by fire" so characteristic of human existence. Just as a clay pot must be fired in the kiln in the final step of its transformation, so too our shortcomings are often transformed in the fiery crucible of life. Yet, in our human weakness, we do not wish to be transformed by fire. Instead, we seek the "easier, softer way" described by AA's *Big Book*.

The Scriptures are clear, however, about the purpose of the inevitable fiery trials of life. In his first letter, the Apostle Peter addressed Christians who were undergoing particularly difficult times in the first century:

> In this you greatly rejoice, though now for a little while you may have had to suffer grief in all kinds of trials. These have come so that your faith—of greater worth than gold, which perishes even though refined by fire—may be proved genuine and may result in praise, glory and honor when Jesus Christ is revealed. (1 Pet. 1:6–7)

Peter says that as we willingly submit to the transforming fire that is part of every Christian's life, our faith can be proved genuine. It is important to note, however, that God requires nothing to know whether our faith is genuine, for he is able to peer deep into our hearts. The fiery trials of life demonstrate to *us* the quality of our faith, so that we may know if our faith is genuine or not.

Another purpose for the trials and sufferings of this life is the production of character. Paul writes:

> . . . we also rejoice in our sufferings, because we know that suffering produces perseverance; perseverance, character; and character, hope. (Rom. 5:3–4)

James adds the following:

> Consider it pure joy, my brothers, whenever you face trials of many kinds, because you know that the testing of your faith develops perseverance. Perseverance must finish its work so that you may be mature and complete, not lacking anything. (James 1:2–4)

The fiery trials of human existence produce mature character and perseverance in those who undergo them. In Step Six, we became entirely ready for God to remove our defects of character. In Step Seven, we willingly submit to the means by which he will purify and transform our shortcomings. In the refining fire of the Christian life, defects are removed and pure character is formed.

Growth toward mature faith and character requires work. Just as the body builder develops huge muscles through the physical exertion of lifting heavy weights, so too the building of strong character requires exertion and work. Nothing grows on Easy Street. There, life atrophies and character dissipates. It is in the crucible of trial and hardship that the pure, twenty-four-karat gold of genuine character is refined.

OUR SHORTCOMINGS

It is especially interesting that Step Seven mentions our *shortcomings,* for that word is very close to a meaning of the word *sin.* In his great psalm of confession, David said, "against you, you only, have I sinned" (Ps. 51:4). In the Septuagint, the Greek version of the Old Testament, the word used for *sin* in this passage is *harmatia,* which means "to miss the mark."[6] This is the sense in which an archer's arrow spends its energy and falls short of the target. The arrow has "missed the mark."

Like David, we too have sinned. We have fallen short of the mark. We have failed to live up to the high standard exacted by God. "For all have sinned and fall short of the glory of God," said Paul (Rom. 3:23). Not only have we failed to reach God's standard, but also we are *incapable,* of our own accord, of living up to God's standard of righteousness. It is as if there is a goal we must reach—and our eternal lives depend on it. Yet our energy is spent and we lay exhausted, far short of the mark. At this point, our Savior Jesus Christ enters the scene and bridges the gap between us and the unattainable mark upon which our eternal lives depend. He has reached the mark *for us* and his achievement is credited vicariously to our account. Now we no longer fall short—we have reached the goal; we have attained the mark, riding, as it were, on the coattails of our Savior.

It is in this sense that God is able to remove our shortcomings. Through the finished work of Jesus Christ on the cross and the crediting of *his* righteousness to *our* accounts, we no longer come up short. We have attained the high standard of righteousness exacted by God; we are fully pleasing and acceptable in his sight. It is because Jesus walked there first that we, as Christians in recovery, may humbly take the seventh step.

CHAPTER XV

Making Amends

STEP EIGHT: *Made a list of all persons we had harmed, and became willing to make amends to them all.*

STEP NINE: *Made direct amends to such people wherever possible, except when to do so would injure them or others.*

Whereas Steps Six and Seven dealt with our vertical relationship with God, Steps Eight and Nine deal with our horizontal relationships, that is, our relationships with our fellow human beings. Recall that the idea of both vertical and horizontal relationships is included in the two great commandments given by our Lord—love God, and love your neighbor as yourself. The cross itself, consisting of both a vertical beam and a horizontal one, symbolizes these relationships.

Steps One through Seven have prepared us for the work to be done in Steps Eight and Nine. In a sense, the first seven steps have provided a framework within which restoration between us and God could occur. The recovering Christian, it is hoped, has also found forgiveness of self within that framework. Restoration between self and God is incomplete, however, in the absence of an honest willingness to restore relationships with others.

MADE A LIST

At first glance, the eighth step may appear deceptively simple. After all, it suggests only that we do two "simple" things: 1) make a list and 2) become willing to do something. Neither task, however, is as simple as we might first think.

Making a list of all persons we have harmed is not a pleasant task; it requires considerable effort and soul-searching. It may conjure up memories of events of which we are now ashamed. Often it will trigger insights into ourselves and our past behaviors that may not have come to light in the moral inventory of Step Four. Yet just as we proceeded at the fourth step with a fearless search into the depths of our hearts, so in Step Eight we continue our courageous journey of discovery.

BECAME WILLING

The second part of this step is also deceptively simple; we are to become willing to make amends. Perhaps we have thought ahead to Step Nine and realized that the actual making of amends (where possible) occurs there and then; thus, the here and now of becoming willing seems easy. The willingness—the honest, sincere willingness—of Step Eight may require, however, the miraculous assistance of God. It is appropriate to humbly ask in prayer that God grant us the willingness needed in this step.

In becoming willing, we are not asked to like it or to relish it. This step suggests that we merely be willing to *commit* to do something. In this case, the task at hand will probably be difficult and unpleasant, for we are asked to come face to face, where possible, with those who have suffered as a result of our addictive lifestyles. Suffice it to say that some of these people will not be happy to see us—much less be sympathetic with our purpose. Nonetheless, we must be willing to make amends to them all.

However, a roadblock may separate us from our willingness: That roadblock is *resentment.* It is naive to believe that all traces of resentment have dissipated through the work done in the previous steps. While God is more than able to miraculously rid us of all resentments, experience shows that resentments are usually remedied only through much personal, spiritual growth. The eighth step provides the opportunity for continued growth by forcing our latent resentments to surface as we remember those persons with whom there has been past conflict.

To speak of resentments toward others may seem inappropriate in the context of Step Eight. After all, we are to address the persons we have harmed, not those who have harmed us. It would seem that our resentments would logically be directed toward those who have harmed us rather than the other way around. In fact, however, it was often our anger and resentment toward others that motivated us to harm them in the first place. Our resentments over injustices, real or imagined, generate behaviors that injure others psychologically and emotionally—and sometimes physically.

When we were engaged in active addiction, our omnipotent egos reigned supreme; his majesty the baby, like a militant tyrant, took what he wanted when he wanted it.

Naturally, many others with whom we came into contact resisted the egocentric demands of our selfish natures. With their insatiable demand for gratification and inability to tolerate frustration, our egos became infuriated toward all who resisted their demands. Through time, that stormy fury festered into poisonous resentment. Our antidote to that festering resentment was to dispense harm and injury to other people in our lives. Now, as Christians in recovery, we must take a hard look at those personal relationships and social interactions that led to our harming others.

For some, the release of resentments is especially difficult because they seem so justified! Perhaps so. Nevertheless, festering resentment poisons the person holding it inside. It is insane to die of poisoning even in the face of justified anger. Hence, all resentments must be released over the course of time so that our systems may be rid of their poisonous effects and renewed spiritual, psychological, and emotional health facilitated.

"The most effective means of overcoming resentment is forgiveness, of ourselves and of others."[1] A tried-and-true means of forgiving others, one already mentioned in this book, is to pray for them—every day for fourteen days. This practice is in keeping with the words of Jesus where he said, "Love your enemies and pray for those who persecute you" (Matt. 5:44). If our Lord asks us to pray even for those who persecute us, surely he expects us to pray for those against whom we hold resentments. The Lord also said:

> Forgive us our debts, as we also have forgiven our debtors . . . For if you forgive men when they sin against you, your heavenly Father will also forgive you. But if you do not forgive men their sins, your Father will not forgive your sins. (Matt. 6:12, 14–15)

THOSE WE HAVE HARMED

Finally, we must consider that portion of Step Eight that reads, "all persons we had harmed." The words are clearly comprehensive; we are to include in our list the names of all people we have harmed emotionally, psychologically, spiritually, physically, financially, sexually, or in whatever other manner we may have injured them. We must include spouses, ex-spouses, and lovers where appropriate. Employers and coworkers must also be included on the list, as well as creditors. We must also include our parents and children; along with spouses, they have suffered the most as a result of a cherished loved one's self-destructive behavior. The list should be as comprehensive as events require. Addiction was like a tornado that ripped through the lives of our families and friends; therefore, it is imperative that we do a thorough job of cleaning up the debris left in the path of the storm so that our rebuilding will be unencumbered.

INTO ACTION

The eighth step is one of preparation. With the ninth comes the action for which we have prepared.

In Step Nine we make amends. This does not mean merely saying "I'm sorry" for wrongs done or injuries inflicted. As writer Pat M. states, "Apologies are not amends. Amends are made by acting differently. I can apologize a hundred times for being late for work and this will not 'mend' the tardiness. Appearing on the job at or before the starting time gives reality to my penitence. What I say about my behavior does not demonstrate change. It is my actions that do this."[2] Step Nine is, therefore, a step of action, one in which we demonstrate our changed behavior toward others.

Apologies, while not sufficient of themselves, are often a necessary part of making amends. In many cases there may be nothing more we can do other than to apologize. For example, there may be no way to restore a marriage. There may have been a divorce as a result of one partner's addictive and adulterous behavior. If the divorced spouse has remarried, then an attempted restoration of the original marriage is inappropriate. A sincere, heartfelt apology, evidenced by continued sobriety and changed behavior, may be all that the recovering addict can offer in restitution for the painful emotional injuries that have occurred. Likewise, in the case of parents, there is no way to make up for years of parental irresponsibility. With the reflection over past behavior that comes with sobriety, there will be deep remorse about the mistreatment and neglect of our children. In many cases, these children may have reached adulthood themselves by the time the parent attains sobriety. Clearly, no apology can restore the lost childhood that resulted from growing up in a home with an addicted parent. The only route to making amends in cases such as this lies in a changed lifestyle that evidences itself in responsible, loving behavior toward those children in a manner appropriate to their current age.

In other cases, there may be opportunity for restitution. If we have cheated someone out of money or property, or perhaps stolen from them, restitution is appropriate. Old debts, long unpaid, might be repaid as a form of restitution or making amends. Restitution, the act of restoring something to its rightful owner, is a biblical principle dating as far back as the days following Israel's exodus from Egypt:

> The Lord said to Moses, "Say to the Israelites: When a man or woman wrongs another in any way and so is unfaithful to the Lord, that person is guilty and must confess the sin

> he has committed. He must make full restitution for his wrong, add one fifth to it and give it all to the person he has wronged. (Num. 5:5–7)

These verses suggest that saying "I'm sorry" is not enough. Where possible and appropriate, every action necessary should be taken to restore relationships and right wrongs.

The restoration of relationships with our fellow human beings also bears upon our spiritual relationship with our heavenly Father. When we are at odds with others as a result of our present or past improprieties, our spiritual relationship with God is hampered; it is as if there is an obstacle standing between us and the Father. There is some unfinished business that must be completed before we can come to God in total freedom.

Jesus was well aware of the interconnectedness of the relationships both with our heavenly Father and our fellow human beings. He said:

> Therefore, if you are offering your gift at the altar and there remember that your brother has something against you, leave your gift there in front of the altar. First go and be reconciled to your brother; then come and offer your gift. (Matt. 5:23–24)

These verses imply that conflictual relationships hamper our worship of God. The restoration of these relationships is so important to our spiritual well-being that Jesus says to go and make amends even if we must walk out in the middle of church services to do it. William Barclay writes:

> Jesus is quite clear about this basic fact—we cannot be right with God until we are right with men; we cannot hope for forgiveness until we have confessed our sin, not only to God, but also to men, and until we have done our best to remove

the practical consequences of it. We sometimes wonder why there is a barrier between us and God; we sometimes wonder why our prayers seem unavailing. The reason may well be that we ourselves have erected that barrier, because we are at variance with our fellow-men, or because we have wronged someone and have done nothing to put things right.[3]

MADE DIRECT AMENDS

Jesus' words indicate that we cannot get around reconciling a conflictual relationship simply by performing an act of service to God; such would be seeking an easier, softer way. Both the Scriptures and Step Nine itself indicate that amends are to be made *directly* to the offended party whenever possible. Making a donation to a church to circumvent the payment of an old debt will not suffice. Teaching children's Sunday school to make up for the neglect of our own children will not work. We must make *direct* amends to those we have harmed. All this, of course, makes Step Nine particularly difficult. If there were a step most of us would choose to skip, this one would probably be it!

WHEREVER POSSIBLE

We must not try to get around the arduous requirement of making direct amends by seeking an easier, softer way.

> We might want to be indirect because it seems easier. For example, it might seem easier just to pay an old debt anonymously by mail. Justice might be done this way, but Step Nine is to help us gain humility, honesty and courage, and that means we need to go directly to the people we have harmed, make direct restitution, and directly admit our wrongs.[4]

As stated earlier, making direct amends may not always be possible. Some of the persons we have harmed may have died, or perhaps we have lost contact with them. In such cases, a vicarious form of restitution may be appropriate: A debt could be repaid to the surviving child of a creditor, for example.

Christians in recovery, however, must remember that the penalty for our sins has been paid by Jesus Christ. In the spiritual sense, we do not have to make up for our past mistakes. If we have sought forgiveness from God and have repented, our sins have been covered by the blood of Jesus Christ. Restitution, however, may be a part of repentance. Recall that repentance means not only a change of our minds but also a change in the direction of our lives. Repentance entails a change in behavior, which brings us right back to making amends: Both repentance and making amends involve action; thus, making amends may be a positive evidence of genuine repentance. We obey the teachings of Jesus not to earn our salvation, but because we love him and wish to follow in his steps. The making of amends is a wonderful way to share the love of Jesus now experienced in our lives.

Yet, if we desire to follow our Lord on the path of love he walked, we will withhold the making of direct amends when to do so would injure others. The often cited example is marital infidelity. If we have been unfaithful to our spouses (and somehow they do not know it), remaining silent may be more loving than confessing the infidelities that occurred during our active addiction. Each of us must honestly examine his or her motives to determine the best course of action. In any case, the motivating factor must be love—not self-protection or the desire to seek an easier way.

When we have done both Steps Eight and Nine, the barriers that have stood in our way are torn down, opening the way to a greater sense of freedom and well-being. It is as if a dark cloud has disappeared from sight, beyond the horizon. The air is cleansed and we breathe more fully and freely, knowing that we have done what we can to repair some of the damage left in the path of the tornado that is addiction. In one sense, our efforts may not have always been successful; but in another sense, they were successful if we honestly tried. After all, we cannot control how other people will receive our attempts at restitution. We do what we can and trust the rest to the care of God.

Once again in the writings of the nineteenth-century English pastor, George MacDonald, we find spiritual insights that bear directly on the journey of recovery. Regarding "duties to an enemy" he wrote:

> It is a very small matter to you whether the man give you your right or not: it is life or death to you whether or not you give him his. Whether he pay you what you count his debt or no, you will be compelled to pay him all you owe him. If you owe him a pound and he you a million, you must pay him the pound whether he pay you the million or not; there is no business parallel here. If, owing you love, he gives you hate, you, owing him love, have yet to pay it.[5]

For our continued recovery and spiritual well-being, our making amends must in no way be contingent upon the other person's response (except when to do so would injure him or her). We must overlook the perceived injustices we have experienced as well as see beyond the innumerable rationalizations we conceive to avoid this step. We must shatter every excuse that hinders the taking of this vital step in the path of recovery. What matters here is not what we are owed, but rather what we owe! Though we cannot control how our efforts at amends will be received by another, this step of restoration remains life or death to us; we must pay our pound though owed a million.

Step Nine is not a one-time act; it is a lifelong process. As we seek to live out this step one day at a time, there is no better creed to follow than that contained in the familiar prayer of St. Francis:

> Lord, make me an instrument of your peace
> Where there is hatred, let me sow love
> Where there is injury, pardon
> Where there is doubt, faith
> Where there is despair, hope
> Where there is darkness, light
> Where there is sadness, joy
> Oh Divine Master, grant that I may not so much seek
> To be consoled, as to console
> To be understood, as to understand
> To be loved, as to love
>
> For
> It is in giving that we receive
> It is in pardoning that we are pardoned
> It is in dying that we are born to eternal life.[6]

CHAPTER XVI

A Daily Struggle

STEP TEN: *Continued to take personal inventory and when we were wrong promptly admitted it.*

Steps Ten through Twelve encourage us to put into *daily* practice the principles learned thus far as we walk the path of recovery in Christ. Beginning with the fourth step, we made a searching and fearless moral inventory of ourselves. Then we admitted to God, to ourselves, and to another human being the exact nature of our wrongs. Our vertical relationship with God became paramount as we were entirely ready to have him remove our defects of character and then humbly asked him to remove our shortcomings. Then our focus shifted to our horizontal relationships with our fellow human beings as we made a list of all persons we had harmed and made the appropriate amends. At Step Ten, we continue to build on the foundation laid in the previous steps.

Step Ten has been described as "a daily visit with Steps Four through Nine" in the program of recovery.[1] Working the steps is a daily struggle; the Christian walk is a daily struggle. These two manners of living are the same, a common path that must be walked one day at a time. The essential nature of the daily struggle is implied in Step Ten as we *continue* to implement the spiritual principles developed thus far. Jesus tells us to take up our cross daily and follow him (*see* Luke 9:23). There can be no vacation, no days off from this struggle. To take time away from the true path of recovery is to invite relapse and regression into active addiction. There can be no return to the old way. Jesus said, "No one who puts his hand to the plow and looks back is fit for service in the kingdom of God" (Luke 9:62).

Daily, ongoing diligence is an essential ingredient for continued recovery. Step Ten implies an attitude of continuous self-reflection and a willingness to reexamine ourselves to make certain we remain on solid footing. Cocky self-assuredness—the certainty that we've got it all figured out—can be deadly. Thus Paul writes, "So, if you think you are standing firm, be careful that you don't fall!" (1 Cor. 10:12).

The need for daily inventory and continued diligence stems from the fact that the "old" man or woman, the egocentric, omnipotent nature—his majesty the baby—dies hard! *All* our character defects and shortcomings, *all* the liabilities uncovered in the Step Four inventory, are directly traceable to that selfish, egocentric human nature that desires to be god in the place of God. His majesty the baby rears up and attempts to sabotage our recovery at every opportunity. Pride, lust, greed, gluttony, envy, deceit, hypocrisy, angry resentment, ad infinitum—are all rooted in the old, sinful nature so often spoken of by the Apostle Paul. He reminds us:

> You were taught, with regard to your former way of life, to put off your old self, which is being corrupted by its deceitful desires; to be made new in the attitude of your minds; and

> to put on the new self, created to be like God in true righteousness and holiness. (Eph. 4:22–24)

Paradoxically, putting off the old self and putting on the new self is *both* a one-time act *and* a daily struggle. When we accept Jesus as our Savior and, at the same time, submit to his Lordship, our old nature dies and a new, redeemed nature rises from the grave to take its place. We are born again! The old has gone, the new has come; we are new creations in Christ. This once-and-for-all change of our status with God, however, is reenacted daily on the stage of our lives as we continually put to death the old sinful self and walk in newness of life. Step Ten, and the two steps that follow it, imply the daily struggle of the new creation against the old.

We dare not become overconfident. We must realize that the old, crucified, egocentric nature may extend a ghostly hand from the grave at any time and pull us under. Paul knew well this daily struggle with the sinful nature. He wrote:

> I know that nothing good lives in me, that is, in my sinful nature. For I have the desire to do what is good, but I cannot carry it out. For what I do is not the good I want to do; no, the evil I do not want to do—this I keep on doing. Now if I do what I do not want to do, it is no longer I who do it, but it is sin living in me that does it. So I find this law at work: When I want to do good, evil is right there with me. (Rom. 7:18–21)

The dangers of overconfidence and the need for continual inventorying are apparent in Paul's words as he describes his struggle with the sinful nature. Fortunately, Paul also describes the solution to his dilemma:

> What a wretched man I am [an example of continual inventorying]! Who will rescue me from this body of death [the

> old, egocentric nature]? Thanks be to God—through Jesus Christ our Lord! . . . he condemned sin in sinful man, in order that the righteous requirements of the law might be fully met in us, who do not live according to the sinful nature but according to the Spirit. (Rom. 7:24–25, 8:3–4)

An attitude of continuous self-reflection and self-examination will reveal our desperate need for God to empower us to overcome the sinful nature. With the supernatural aid of Jesus Christ, working through the Holy Spirit, we can overcome that old egocentricity and remain on the path of recovery.

THINKING, FEELING, DOING

As we continue to take personal inventory, we will diligently look for any manifestation of the old sinful nature, knowing that even with no less a saint than Paul, its manifestations will be all too frequent. Each of us must determine individually where to focus our attention as we continually monitor ourselves for evidence of the omnipotent, egocentric nature—his majesty the baby. An occasional review of the written Step Four inventory may be helpful.

In more general terms, we must monitor our thoughts, feelings, and behaviors. The field of cognitive psychology has demonstrated that our feelings and actions are greatly influenced by what we think. Daily monitoring of thoughts is important so as to avoid the "stinking thinking" often described in Twelve-Step meetings. Jesus said, "For out of the heart come evil thoughts, murder, adultery, sexual immorality, theft, false testimony, slander" (Matt. 15:19). Paul knew the importance of having our minds in the right place:

> Those who live according to the sinful nature have their minds set on what that nature desires; but those who live in accordance with the Spirit have their minds set on what the Spirit desires. The mind of sinful man is death, but the mind controlled by the Spirit is life and peace. (Rom. 8:5–6)

An especially dangerous form of aberrant thinking, and one which must be continually monitored by those of us in recovery, is resentment. Resentments, even those supposedly justified ones, poison our minds and brew seething emotions and destructive behaviors. They must be dealt with promptly or their poisonous effects will rapidly overcome us.

Of course, resentful thoughts are not the only kind of thoughts that are dangerous or harmful to recovery. Prideful, arrogant, and conceited thoughts litter the path to relapse. Lustful thoughts, those of an explicitly sexual nature, shatter the serenity and peace of mind that accompanies recovery. All these forms of aberrant thinking rob us of "the peace of God that transcends all understanding" (Phil. 4:7).

As we monitor daily our thoughts, we do well to heed Paul's words to the Christians at Philippi:

> Whatever is true, whatever is noble, whatever is right, whatever is pure, whatever is lovely, whatever is admirable—if anything is excellent or praiseworthy—think about such things. (Phil. 4:8)

Another area for daily inventory is feelings. Feelings long medicated by chemicals or compulsive behaviors are difficult to identify. Anger and fear, for example, two emotions that are physiologically quite similar, are often difficult for us to differentiate. As recovery progresses and feelings begin to surface, they can become motivators for innumerable behaviors. Anger, for example, may be either a useful emotion that prompts us to defend our boundaries, or it may be a destructive emotion that leads to seeking vengeance. We must continually monitor both the thoughts and behaviors generated by our feelings.

Consider the words of Jesus regarding anger: "You have heard that it was said to the people long ago, 'Do not murder, and anyone who murders will be subject to judgment.' But I tell you that anyone who is angry with his brother will be subject to judgment" (Matt. 5:21–22a). Here Jesus is speaking of a kind of anger that is "inveterate. . . . It is the long-lived anger; it is the anger of the man who nurses his wrath to keep it warm; it is the anger over which a person broods, and which he will not allow to die. That anger is liable to the judgment court . . . So Jesus forbids forever the anger which broods, the anger which will not forget, the anger which refuses to be pacified, the anger which seeks revenge."[2]

As illustrated by this example, the motivation and purpose of our emotions must be evaluated through daily inventorying and self-reflection. Remember that emotions in and of themselves are neither good nor bad, just as the thoughts and behaviors prompted by them may be either good or bad. We must continually seek the searching light of the Son to illuminate the true nature of our emotions.

Finally, we must constantly monitor our actions or behaviors to see that they are neither offensive to God, to ourselves, or to those around us. If we reflect upon our thoughts and emotions, we may prevent the occurrence of harmful actions on our parts. If we are conscious of the true nature of our thoughts and feelings—that is, if we have overcome denial and self-deception—many of the selfish, harmful behaviors of our addictive pasts need not occur in recovery.

Just as we did in the Step Four inventory, in Step Ten we also must follow the example of the Psalmist and pray to our heavenly Father: "Search me, O God, and know my heart; test me and know my anxious thoughts. See if there is any offensive way in me, and lead me in the way everlasting" (Ps. 139:23–24).

In summary, the continued, daily inventory of Step Ten is, in reality, an ongoing search-and-destroy mission whose goal is to root out and put to death every manifestation of the sinful, egocentric nature that was at the heart of our addiction.

PROMPTNESS

Step Ten suggests that when we are wrong, we promptly admit it. The longer we delay in admitting a wrong and making the necessary amends, the more likely we are to concoct a variety of excuses for forgetting the whole thing! The Scriptures bear witness to the importance of the timely rectification of wrongs; Jesus said:

> Settle matters quickly with your adversary who is taking you to court. Do it while you are still with him on the way, or he may hand you over to the judge . . . and you may be thrown into prison. I tell you the truth, you will not get out until you have paid the last penny. (Matt. 5:25–26)

Commenting on this passage, William Barclay writes: "When personal relations go wrong, in nine cases out of ten immediate action will mend them; but if that immediate action is not taken, they will continue to deteriorate, and the bitterness will spread in an ever-widening circle."[3]

The principle of timely rectification of wrongs is seen also in the writings of Paul. He said: "'In your anger do not sin':

Do not let the sun go down while you are still angry, and do not give the devil a foothold" (Eph. 4:26–27). Like Jesus, the Apostle Paul admonishes us to settle matters quickly before the situation worsens. We must not allow pride or even being "in the right" to hinder the prompt admission of wrongs and the offering of the amends necessary to rectify them.

"Good Tenth Stepping brings its own rewards," writes Mel B., a fellow traveler on the road of recovery. He continues, "The most important benefit of this step is that it strengthens and protects one's sobriety. It also brings rewards in several other areas."[4] Personal relationships improve with "good Tenth Stepping." The prompt admission of wrongs usually corrects misunderstandings in the initial stages, before the situation worsens. There is "freedom from fear of 'being found out.'" When we promptly admit our wrongs as a result of daily inventorying, we no longer feel the need to "maintain a facade" or wear a mask in hopes that others will perceive us as something other than what we are. Guilt is a common consequence of a refusal to admit wrongs. Good tenth stepping alleviates that guilt. Finally, "one surprising benefit of admitting one's wrongs is becoming able to help others make similar admissions . . . if someone practices self-honesty, [others] can sense this and will seek out that person for help with [their] problems."[5]

CHAPTER XVII

Prayer and Meditation

STEP ELEVEN: *Sought through prayer and meditation to improve our conscious contact with God,* as we understood Him, *praying only for knowledge of his will for us and the power to carry that out.*

The eleventh step is another step of action, for it introduces the activities of prayer and meditation. First and foremost, however, it is a step of seeking—we "sought" to do something. Using the tools of prayer and meditation, we seek to improve our conscious contact with God. Implied within this step, of course, is the assumption that we have already made contact with God.

Step Eleven clearly demonstrates the importance of taking the steps as they come. This step can only be taken if Step Three has been taken. In the third step, we surrendered our will and our lives to God's care. The egocentric, selfish nature inherent from birth was dethroned and a new King, Jesus Christ, was enthroned in our lives. At Step Eleven, we seek to improve our conscious contact with our new Ruler so that we may better understand his will for us. If we are still operating under the tyrannical rule of self-will, we cannot seek the improved knowledge of God's will in our lives called for in Step Eleven.

For the Christian in recovery, Jesus Christ is the cornerstone of the program (*see* Eph. 2:19–20). He, and only he, is "God as we understand him." No other higher power can provide the *power* and support called for in Step Eleven. The eleventh step is a roadblock for those who have trivialized the concept of a higher power. This step not only describes a higher power we can pray to (and who, presumably, will hear our prayers) but also a higher power who can give us the power to know and carry out his will.

As we take root ever deeper into the good soil of the Twelve Steps, it becomes even more clear that we must have real light to grow. We require the light of the Son of God for our spiritual nourishment so that we may blossom in health and recovery. No phony or trivialized higher power can give us the light we need to grow into psychological, emotional, and spiritual maturity. For those who wish to grow straight and tall in their program of recovery, there can be no god but God and no higher power but Jesus Christ. To him be the glory both now and forever!

LORD, TEACH US TO PRAY

An essential tool for improving our conscious contact with God is prayer. Many people coming into Twelve-Step programs, however, are uncomfortable with prayer. They have many misconceptions about this form of spiritual communication.

Even Jesus' disciples seemed to misunderstand this form of communing with God. One of them finally asked him, "Lord, teach us to pray" (Luke 11:1). Included in Jesus' answer to that request is what is usually referred to as "the Lord's Prayer." Jesus said (using Matthew's version):

> "This, then, is how you should pray:
>
> "'Our Father in heaven,
> hallowed be your name,
> your kingdom come,
> your will be done
> on earth as it is in heaven.
> Give us today our daily bread.
> Forgive us our debts,
> as we also have forgiven our debtors.
> And lead us not into temptation,
> but deliver us from the evil one.'"
>
> Some manuscripts add:
>
> "for yours is the kingdom
> and the power and the glory forever. Amen."
> (Matt. 6:9–13)

This prayer is often recited at the close of Twelve-Step meetings. It is useful not only as a memorized prayer, but also as a *model* for prayer. After all, Jesus did not instruct us always to pray this prayer; he said, rather, "This, then, is *how* you should pray."

Before examining this prayer in some detail, however, notice a couple of things about it in general. Note especially that it is a simple prayer; it is not couched in impressive words of theological grandeur; it is not ornate. Jesus did not use this opportunity to show us his ability to pray slick, canned prayers, filled with flowering oratory designed more to impress listeners than to address God. Instead, notice that this model prayer is more like a straightforward address of a son or daughter to his or her Father. I would be remiss, however, if I did not add that, though this prayer is simple and straightforward, it is also profound, for Jesus covers a lot of ground in the relatively few words of this prayer. Let's look at the prayer in some detail.

Jesus begins by addressing our heavenly "Father." This is the loving Father who is waiting to hear our prayers, the Father who *delights* in our prayers. The prayers of the saints—God's people—are to him like "golden bowls full of incense" (Rev. 5:8d), having a delightful aroma, one in which he takes great pleasure. As we offer our prayers up to him, we should remember that he is the same Father who, as in the story of the Prodigal Son, is waiting to shower us with love and understanding as we approach his throne room in prayer.

Jesus then prays, "Hallowed be your name." Something that is hallowed is *sacred* or *revered.* We, as Christians, are to hold God's name as something sacred, much as did the early Hebrews who esteemed God's name so highly that they didn't even say it! We must not use His name in a trivial or disrespectful manner.

Jesus then prays for the coming of God's kingdom to the earth. As Christians in recovery, we have a unique opportunity to spread the message of that kingdom to our non-Christian friends in recovery. Further, as we consider the pain and misery that is pervasive in this world, we Christians can look forward to the physical, literal return of Jesus Christ, in power and glory, to usher in the reign of God throughout the earth. Then, as every knee bows and every tongue confesses Jesus as Lord, the weeping and suffering will end under the direct, physical rulership of the King of kings.

Jesus instructs us to pray that God's will be done. The appropriate place for each of us to seek God's will is in our own lives. This is, of course, the message of Step Three; God's will becomes the guiding force in our lives. Our prayers are a means by which we seek the knowledge of God's will for us, as Step Eleven plainly teaches.

Next, the Lord instructs us to pray that God provide us our daily bread. There is so much that can be said about this subject, but for the present purpose, I will be brief. Jesus' teaching about prayer is in harmony with his instruction to "Seek first his kingdom and his righteousness, and all these things [food, clothing, and so forth] will be given to you as well" (Matt. 6:33). Jesus did not say "seek first your daily bread." In the Lord's prayer, he did not put that important topic first, either; thus, his teaching, as always, is consistent. The Lord instructs us to pray for other things before praying for our daily needs; nonetheless, praying for our daily bread is included in his teaching on prayer. The important point is that we are to look to our heavenly Father to supply our daily needs. Just as he rained down manna from heaven, one day's worth at a time, to the ancient Israelites as they wandered in the wilderness for forty years, so too will he provide for the needs of those who seek him first—one day at a time. This does not mean, however, that we sit on our rears with our mouths open and wait for God to feed us in the same way he provides for birds; it does mean that we do what we can and leave the rest to God. We plow the field God gives us to plow, but we rely on God to send the sunshine and the rain needed to make the crop grow. For the Christian, then, our heavenly Father must be looked to as the ultimate source of our provision and the sustainer of our lives.

One final point about this part of the prayer is that Jesus is teaching us to live "one day at a time," a very familiar slogan to most Twelve-Steppers. We are to ask God for what we need *today* and leave it at that. In all fairness, however, I must add that this manner of living must be learned over a considerable length of time—at least, that has been the case for me.

Jesus next instructs us to ask for God's forgiveness of our sins (debts) as we forgive those who have injured us. This part of the prayer is in keeping with the Twelve-Step wisdom that instructs us to pray for those against whom we hold resentments. As we remember that God is very willing to forgive us our shortcomings, we must also remember that he expects us to do the same for others.

Finally, in this model prayer, Jesus instructs us to pray that we be kept from temptation and out of the clutches of the Evil One—Satan.

A different version of this prayer is cited in Luke, chapter 11. Since the wording of the two versions is slightly different, it is safe to assume that the ideas contained in the Lord's Prayer are more important than the exact wording. Following Luke's version, there is a short parable that introduces the idea of persistence or boldness in prayer (*see* Luke 11:5–8). Jesus instructs us to be persistent in our prayers, to keep on asking until we have received an answer—either yes or no. Persistence in prayer is more of a matter of our faith than of God's ability to hear.

Thus Jesus himself has provided us a model for prayer. This does not mean that we are to pray in this exact manner every time we pray; however, it is a useful framework for organizing our thoughts and petitions to God.

Jesus not only gave us a model for prayer but he also served as an example in this regard, for prayer was an important part of his life. He often rose early in the morning and went to a solitary place to pray (*see* Mark 1:35). Sometimes, he even spent the night praying to his heavenly Father (*see* Luke 6:12). Does this mean, then, that all our prayers must be premeditated acts wherein we ceremoniously seek a solitary place to be alone and formally speak with God? By no means! Our prayers may take an infinite variety of forms and occur in myriad places and situations.

Prayer is simply talking to God. The words may or may not be spoken aloud. We should talk to God in the way a grown-up child talks to a loving parent or in the way a good and faithful servant speaks to a loving, caring master. We need not pray with lofty, sanctimonious words—no "thees" or "thous" are necessary. Our prayers should be real and straight from the heart.

One of my favorite times and places to pray is in the morning, sitting at the table with a freshly poured cup of coffee on hand. I spend some time thinking about God and his will for my life and I talk to him about whatever is on my mind. I also love to walk in the woods and talk to God as I am walking. In that setting I am especially cognizant of his role as Creator as the beauty of the outdoors moves me to thank him for his creation. Another place I love to visit for prayer is a beautiful cathedral in my town. The stained glass, the altar with the cross, and the dark, rich wood throughout create a feeling of sacred space that is especially conducive to my communing with my Father in heaven. And yes, sometimes I kneel beside my bed and pray to God there.

C.S. Lewis, one of the great Christian writers of this century, had his own thoughts about where and when to pray. He said that he would rather pray on a crowded train or while sitting on a park bench than reserve his prayers for bedtime when he was too tired to concentrate.[1] One may pray while driving a car or taking a walk; the time and place are far less important than prayer itself. George MacDonald said, "Never wait for fitter time or place to talk to Him. To wait till thou go to church or to thy closet is to make Him wait. He will listen as thou walkest."[2]

Prayer may also be an ongoing conversation with God. On some days, I talk to him almost constantly. It is as if he is there beside me (which he is!) and I am carrying on a conversation with him. The prayer may be a quick thought—not even a complete sentence—or it may be a series of thoughts, ideas, questions, or wishes. The Scripture instructs us to "pray continually" (1 Thess. 5:17). This is only possible if God is constantly in our thoughts. A continuing awareness of God's presence in our daily lives facilitates constant conversation with him. In this regard, author and businessman Pat Morley offers a helpful insight: "Who do you talk to when you are mulling over a problem or daydreaming away the time? If you find yourself talking to yourself, stop. Talk it over with the Lord instead. Let Him be your soul mate. Anytime you catch yourself talking to yourself, redirect the conversation to God. That's what it means to pray without ceasing."[3] We "pray without ceasing," or pray continually, when we are constantly mindful of God's presence and direct our thoughts toward him.

Sometimes, however, we wish to talk to God, but simply do not know what to say. A problem may be so overwhelming and confusing that we don't know what to pray about. Perhaps we feel the need to make a request of God but are unsure of what to ask for. At times such as these, it is enough to bow our heads and allow the Holy Spirit to intercede for us "with groans that words cannot express." Even when we are not sure how and what to pray, God, through the work of the Holy Spirit, will supply even that need (*see* Rom. 8:26–27). Pat Morley calls this the "inarticulate need." He writes:

> Have you ever been so overwhelmed by life that you didn't even know where to begin praying? What do we say to Him? If we say nothing at all, He will understand our need

> perfectly. The inarticulate need that is still unknown to us is transparent to the Lord.[4]

Even when we are so overwhelmed by life that we cannot find the right words, the Holy Spirit will pray for us.

As stated previously, our prayers need only be simple and direct communications to our loving Father in heaven. As a testimony to the fact that a prayer need not blossom in the glory of pompous theological jargon to be effective, but rather need be only simple and heartfelt, read the following parable of Jesus—and be certain to notice which prayer was heard.

> To some who were confident of their own righteousness and looked down on everybody else, Jesus told this parable:
>
> "Two men went up to the temple to pray, one a Pharisee and the other a tax collector. The Pharisee stood up and prayed about himself: 'God, I thank you that I am not like other men—robbers, evildoers, adulterers—or even like this tax collector. I fast twice a week and give a tenth of all I get.'
>
> "But the tax collector stood at a distance. He would not even look up to heaven, but beat his breast and said, 'God, have mercy on me, a sinner.'
>
> "I tell you that this man, rather than the other, went home justified before God. For everyone who exalts himself will be humbled, and he who humbles himself will be exalted." (Luke 18:9–14)

Several points in this parable must not escape our attention. Two men are praying in the story. One is a Pharisee, a religious leader of the day, a man considered by the Jews as the epitome of righteousness and godliness. The other man praying is a tax collector, or as the Jews usually put it, a "despised" tax collector. Men of his profession were regarded by the Jews as traitors, agents of the oppressive

Roman government, and were thoroughly hated by their people. Yet it is the prayer of this "despised" tax collector that is heard rather than the prayer of the self-righteous, sanctimonious Pharisee. God does not look on outward appearances as men do; God looks on the heart. The tax collector knew he was a sinner and sincerely sought God's mercy—and he received it. The Pharisee was so hung up on himself that he could not see his need for forgiveness—and he received none!

We Christians in recovery must remember that God is very willing to forgive us, even though we may have done things that some would regard as "despised." It is not the sanctimoniously religious person or the goody two shoes that receives God's grace; it is the sincerely penitent heart that never fails to receive his mercy. "A broken and contrite heart, O God, you will not despise" (Ps. 51:17).

MEDITATION

Meditation is more popular in Twelve-Step circles than in the community of evangelical Christians. For many Christians, the concept of meditation conjures up images of yogis sitting in Zen-like positions amidst thick clouds of incense. Meditation, however, is a *biblical* concept. David, for example, meditated on the law of the Lord day and night (*see* Ps. 1:1–2).

To meditate, according to *Webster's Ninth Collegiate Dictionary,* is "to focus one's thoughts on; to reflect on or ponder over." We see this again in the Psalms where David writes, "On my bed I remember you [God]; I think of you through the watches of the night" (Ps. 63:6). Like David, it is highly desirable for Christians in recovery to focus their thoughts on God and his ways.

As stated in Step Eleven, the purpose of meditation is "to improve our conscious contact with God." The only requirements for meditation are a willing heart and a quiet place with no distractions. In this quiet time, we should focus on God, on his attributes, and on his will for our lives. It is a time not only of focusing on God, but also of peering deep into our own hearts to see what desires God has placed there.

A meditative quiet time using a devotional aid is an excellent way to start the day. This practice enables us to begin our day not only in a positive manner, but more importantly, with a sense of *connectedness* to our heavenly Father. Moreover, it is not at all unusual to discover that the devotional material we read at the beginning of a given day is exactly what we need for a particular situation or spiritual decision with which we are presently confronted.

The line between prayer and meditation is a blurred one. As we meditate or focus our thoughts on spiritual matters, we will naturally pray about them as well. Often, these prayers will be informal conversations with God. Both these practices—prayer and meditation—will improve our conscious contact with him. Even more, they provide the moments of peace and quietness so necessary for that still, small voice of God to enter our consciousness, for he is far more likely to speak to us in moments of quiet prayer and meditation than he is to roar at us from a mountaintop.

A word of caution is warranted, however, regarding a daily quiet time. The reality of daily life, especially the chaos of the morning rush—getting dressed, getting kids off to school, preparing sack lunches, and other duties—makes an early morning quiet time difficult if not impossible. If hectic schedules make morning quiet times unfeasible, take fifteen minutes of a lunch break to get alone with God. Or perhaps a short walk after dinner will accomplish the goal of focusing one's thoughts on God and his will for one's life. The practice of prayer and meditation is more important than issues around the time of day or place where the practice is conducted. Unfortunately, "the quiet time often becomes a hollow convention of religious structure, instead of a holy meeting with the personal Christ."[5] Instead of drinking deeply of God's word, we read a couple of quick verses then rush out the door to work. The quiet time becomes just another "perfunctory duty of the Christian life, another activity to verify our Christianity to ourselves," says Pat Morley.[6] To borrow the words of George MacDonald, engage in prayer and meditation when these practices can be done out of "the strength of love" rather than "the effort of duty."[7] In other words, seek time alone with God when you thirst for it, not just to fulfill a legalistic obligation or to assuage the tyrannical demands of a needlessly guilty conscience.

For those who truly thirst for God, who desire to draw closer to him, prayer and meditation will become important parts of their lives. Thus, our Father admonishes us to "be still, and know that I am God" (Ps. 46:10). It is vital to recovery to have regular times away from the demanding distractions of daily life that so easily keep us focused on everything but God. Make prayer and meditation top priorities in your life and your recovery will be immeasurably enhanced by them.

> May the words of my mouth and the meditation
> of my heart
> be pleasing in your sight,
> O Lord, my Rock and my Redeemer.
> (Ps. 19:14)

CHAPTER XVIII

Knowledge of His Will

STEP ELEVEN: *Sought through prayer and meditation to improve our conscious contact with God,* as we understood Him, *praying only for knowledge of his will for us and the power to carry that out.*

As we address this portion of Step Eleven, it becomes increasingly clear that the basic foundation for recovery and surrender to God must have been laid at Step Three. Unless we have turned our will and our lives over to the care of God, we will have little interest in "praying only for knowledge of his will for us and the power to carry that out." If his majesty the baby, the omnipotent egocentricity, has not been thoroughly buried, it will continue to raise its ugly head and assert its claim in our lives, along with its selfish demands for its own way.

It is clear, though, that Jesus taught us to pray only for the will of the Father. As we saw in Chapter 17, the Lord taught us to pray, "Your will be done." Jesus further set the example for us as he agonized in prayer in the Garden of Gethsemane the night before his crucifixion. As he contemplated the horrible ordeal he was soon to undergo, He prayed,

"My Father, if it is possible, may this cup be taken from me. Yet not as I will, but as you will" (Matt. 26:39).

Jesus was *willing* to turn his life over to the care of the heavenly Father. Most of us, however, tend to be *willful* rather than willing. To be *willing* means "Your will be done, God; I place my trust in your guidance and wisdom." *Willful* means "My will be done; I know what is best for me." Prior to recovery, we were willful. We did as we pleased virtually whenever we pleased. In our egocentric demand for self-gratification, many of us trampled everyone and everything in our way to get what we wanted. Recovery, on the other hand, demands *willingness.* Rather than asserting "I, me, mine," willingness desires that God's "will be done on earth as it is in heaven." Recovery is the gradual process of moving from willful to willing.

THE DESIRES OF YOUR HEART

At this point then, the important question for those of us who are willing is, "How can we know God's will for our lives?" The answer to that question may be as surprising as it is controversial.

There is an easily misunderstood scripture that reads, "Delight yourself in the Lord and he will give you the desires of your heart" (Ps. 37:4). Proponents of the health-and-wealth gospel twist this scripture to mean that if I want a new Mercedes-Benz, then God is obligated to deliver it to me. Businessman Pat Morley once held this mistaken view of this verse. He writes, "I claimed this verse as a promise for a business deal here and a possession there. I delighted in the Lord and waited patiently for Him to shower me with my heart's desires."[1] The problem lay in a misunderstanding of "delight." The word *delight* comes from a Hebrew word that means "soft or pliable." Morley finally realized that "to 'delight' in the Lord is to be clay in the potter's hands, to come humbly without heavy demands, to come eager to know the God who is and not the God we want, to come anxious for God to 'make me' rather than for Him to 'give me'."[2]

As he honestly and genuinely began to seek God's will for his life, a miraculous transformation began within his heart. Morley continues:

> As I surrendered my expectations and 'delighted' in Him, the desires of my heart began to change. Through my newfound pliability, He changed my desires by making His desires come alive in me. Over time, His desires actually became my desires. And when my desires were one with His desires in a given area, He would grant them. He granted them because they were actually His desires (His will) now alive in me as the delight of my own heart.[3]

Thus, as Morley increasingly surrendered his will to God's will, there grew an increasing similarity between his will and God's will.

As we surrender our lives to Jesus Christ, or in Twelve-Step terminology, as we turn our will and our lives over to the care of God, a miraculous transformation begins in our hearts. God begins to change our desires so that the things that once seemed so important, financial success or social prestige for example, no longer seem as important as they once did. In other words, our priorities change. We cease chasing after all those things that the "pagans" seek, to use Jesus' words. Wealth and riches, social prestige and fame, fancy cars, titles and positions, power over others—all such things begin to lose their attraction for us. We become less interested in the things of the world and more interested in the things of God. The material realm decreases in importance as the spiritual realm increases in importance. If our hearts are committed to Christ, then a new set of desires develops within us. These desires are put there by God to motivate us to follow the path he wishes us to follow.

The Apostle Paul speaks of "Christ in you" (Col. 1:27), and in another place he says, "Christ lives in me" (Gal. 2:20). If Jesus Christ lives and reigns in your heart, then the desires of your heart are Christ's desires alive in you. Yet, paradoxically, they are also your desires. The two become one and the same. Thus to know what he wants for you, it is not necessary to look outside of yourself to find it; instead, look inside, to the desires of your own heart, and you will find God's will for your life. The heart that is truly dedicated to the Lord is trustworthy. Therefore, if you have given your heart to him, then *follow the longings of your heart* and you will go where the Lord wants you to go. Jesus, the Lord of your heart, is directing your desires; therefore, listen to what your heart is telling you.

The Inevitable Objections

I would be remiss, however, if I did not attempt to address some objections that will surely arise in light of what I have written. Some in Christian circles will argue that it is foolish for one to trust his or her own heart. They will cynically remind us that "the heart is deceitful above all things" (Jer. 17:9). Others will argue that all this is selfish; they will say that we must deny ourselves, that we must sacrifice all human desires to the service of God. In all fairness, the long list of Christian martyrs does bear solemn testimony to the fact that God sometimes requires the ultimate sacrifice for his service.

Nevertheless, everything I have written in this regard applies *only* to those who have presented themselves as "living sacrifices" to God (Rom. 12:1), who have dedicated their hearts to the service of the Lord. To deny ourselves and follow Jesus means far more than merely foregoing this or that pleasure to demonstrate our Christianity. As followers of Jesus, we deny our right to ourselves. We were bought at a price; we are no longer our own (*see* 1 Cor. 6:19–20). We surrender our lives to him—completely.

Yet it is in losing our life to him that we find it. Our former stony, hardened hearts that were centered in self rather than God are removed and are replaced with a new heart dedicated to God (*see* Ezek. 36:26), and it is the desires of that new heart that we may freely follow. If Jesus lives in your heart, then the desires of your heart are his desires; thus, the right thing to do is to follow them. We take up our cross daily and follow Jesus by walking the path he sets before us. When we walk *that* path, we discover it is the one we desired to follow all along. It is the true path, the one God has set for each of us to walk.

Nonetheless, other objections will undoubtedly arise, for it is not just the Bible thumpers who will take issue with what I have written in this regard; many Twelve-Step participants will also be critical. They will cite the overabundance of Twelve-Step literature that asserts that no addict, recovering or not, knows what's good for him or her. Others will chalk up what I have written to "alcoholic grandiosity" or "stinking thinking."

To be sure, my friends, what I have written is emphatically not for "babes in Christ" or newcomers to the Twelve Steps. Those new in recovery usually do not know what is best for them. But there comes a time when spiritual maturity requires that we *transcend* all forms of dogma—whether it be the dogma of the institutionalized Church or the dogma that has developed around the Twelve Steps.

Each of us is a unique creation, capable of fulfilling a function in the body of Christ that no other can fill. That function can only be fulfilled when we allow God to transform us into the unique vessels that each Christian is destined to become. We can never realize our unique potential in Christ by copying someone else or playing by someone else's rules. We must set out upon our individual spiritual journeys and be willing to walk them alone if necessary. All around will be those who insist that we must remain within the safe confines of the village compound, that we dare not set out on our own, individual paths. They will quote Scripture or cite *The Big Book* to prove that we dare not become unique creations in Christ. Yet spiritual maturity is charting our own course, carving our own path, walking our own walk with God.

The spiritually mature follow no one but Christ, and they do so by following the desires of their own Christ-filled hearts. No wonder Jesus said, "For wide is the gate and broad is the road that leads to destruction, and *many* enter through it. But small is the gate and narrow is the road that leads to life, and only a *few* find it" (Matt. 7:13). As my friend Ken Gilburth puts it, "the true path is a lonely backpacking trail through the 'wild-erness,' yet most people are traveling an eight-lane interstate." As Christians who are growing in the grace and knowledge of our Lord Jesus Christ, we need not be afraid to follow the desires of our own hearts, which is the only way to abundant life.

In summary, if Christ be in you, if he is Lord of your heart, then your heart's desires are his desires for you. To know his will, then, simply follow the desires of your own heart.

BREAD AND STONE

What about making specific requests of God, however? Is there latitude in God's will for us, or is his perfect will a razor's edge with no room for us to move about?

By now, some readers may think that I view God as some sort of cosmic Santa Claus who is going to give us everything we ask for. I assure you, that is not the case! While the overarching desires of the Christian's heart are put there by God, that does not mean that he will grant every specific request we make of him.

God is our Father—our loving, heavenly Father. As such, he is anxious to give good things to us. Jesus said:

> Ask and it will be given to you; seek and you will find; knock and the door will be opened to you. For everyone who asks receives; he who seeks finds; and to him who knocks, the door will be opened. Which of you, if his son asks for bread, will give him a stone? Or if he asks for a fish, will give him a snake? If you, then, though you are evil, know how to give good gifts to your children, how much more will your Father in heaven give good gifts to those who ask him! (Matt. 7:7–11)

Just as human parents desire to provide good things for their children, how much more does our Heavenly Father desire to give good gifts to his children. "Ask for any one of these things that is good for you, that is for the salvation of your soul, your ultimate perfection, anything that brings you nearer to God and enlarges your life and is thoroughly good for you, and He will give it to you," writes Dr. Martin Lloyd-Jones.[4]

Luke's version of the previous passage reads, "how much more will your Father in heaven give the Holy Spirit to those who ask" (*see* Luke 11:9–13). The "good things" that God desires to give us are any things that produce the fruit of the Spirit in our lives—love, joy, peace, patience, kindness, goodness, faithfulness, gentleness, self-control.[5] God desires to grant every request that will enhance our spirituality in this sense, regardless of what the request is.

Sometimes, however, the things we ask of God are not good things. In our finitude, we are certain we want this job or that promotion; we are totally convinced that we want this relationship to work out; we know that we will be happy for the rest of our lives if only we can move to this or that place. Yet experience shows that we do not always know what we want, especially in the early stages of recovery (and often later on as well). How many of us have asked God for something, certain that it was just what we needed, only to realize months or years later that his refusal to grant our request was a blessing—we just didn't know it at the time. God will not give us a snake just because we think it is a fish! Because he loves us, he will answer "no" when it is in our best interests.

Occasionally, however, as God strives to teach us that he knows what is best for us, he will grant our inappropriate wishes. For example, we pray, "God, I know this is what I want. I know what is best for me. Just cooperate, God, OK?" Doesn't that sound familiar? Since, in our finite human understanding, we are so certain we know what we want, God may allow us to have what we ask for. It is in this context that we hear the often cited Twelve-Step slogan, "Careful what you ask for, you might get it!" To facilitate our understanding that we, in fact, do not always know what is best for us in each and every circumstance, God sometimes will grant our requests; this has been called "corrective granting." Pastor George MacDonald describes it as follows:

> Even such as ask amiss may sometimes have their prayers answered. The Father will never give the child a stone that asks for bread; but I am not sure that He will never give the child a stone that asks for a stone. If the Father says, "My child, that is a stone; it is no bread," and the child answer, "I am sure it is bread; I want it," may it not be well that he should try his "bread"?[6]

We see stone and think it is bread; then, in our willfulness, we insist upon having our "bread." God sometimes grants our requests to teach us the difference between bread and stone. Yet even though God will sometimes give us a stone when we ask for a stone so that we can learn the difference between stone and bread, he will never give us a stone when we ask for bread. The problem is that we often don't know the difference between stone and bread or snakes and fish. Thankfully, God does.

A Matter of Motives

We often complain that God does not answer our prayers. What we usually mean is that we didn't get what we asked for. The reason for God's refusal to answer our requests is plain: We ask out of wrong motives. When our requests are not made out of a desire to serve God, but rather are made from a desire to serve self to the exclusion of God, he refuses to grant our petitions. The Apostle James wrote, "When you ask, you do not receive, because you ask with wrong motives, that you may spend what you get on your pleasures" (James 4:3). Here is a common reason that our prayers are not answered: Our motives for asking are purely selfish. In the language of the old King James Version of the Bible, we ask so that we may "consume it upon our lusts." The omnipotent, egocentric nature—his majesty the baby—is back on the throne; we've taken it back, rather than turned it over. We are running our own show again, rather than submitting our will and our lives to God. With God banished from our hearts, the desires of our hearts are no longer in line with God's will. Thus our prayers and requests are not answered.

When our hearts are totally dedicated to God, however, we are in an entirely different position. When we seek God's will first, we need not hesitate to make our requests known to God because everything is framed in the context of "Your will be done." Paul wrote:

> Do not be anxious about anything, but in everything, by prayer and petition, with thanksgiving, present your requests to God. (Phil. 4:6)

In making our specific requests to God, we must thoroughly examine our own motives. Do we ask so that we may spend it on our pleasures or do we "seek first the Kingdom of God and his righteousness"? The Christian whose heart is dedicated to God will less likely pray, "God, I want this ______" than pray, "God, what would you have me do about ______." When we are mindful of him to whom our prayers are directed, and when our hearts are submitted to God and his rulership first, we need not hesitate to make our specific requests known to him; our heavenly Father will then grant us the good things for which we ask him.

> He who seeks the Father more than anything He can give, is likely to have what He asks, for he is not likely to ask amiss.[7]

AND THE POWER TO CARRY THAT OUT

Those who have trivialized the concept of a higher power run into real trouble at this part of Step Eleven ("praying only for knowledge of His will for us and the power to carry that out"). Those whose higher power is a pickup truck, a lucky charm, or a block of wood or stone will find themselves groping unaided into recovery. In fact, what they call recovery may be nothing more than a white-knuckled attempt at abstinence. If we are to experience real recovery and the consequent spirituality that inevitably accompanies it, we must receive genuine *power* to strengthen us and make prolonged abstinence possible. For Christians in recovery, that real Power is available in the person of the Holy Spirit.

After his resurrection, the Lord told the disciples, "You will receive power when the Holy Spirit comes on you" (Acts 1:8). Later, after Jesus had ascended into heaven,

> [The disciples] were all together in one place. Suddenly a sound like the blowing of a violent wind came from heaven and filled the whole house where they were sitting. They saw what seemed to be tongues of fire that separated and came to rest on each of them. All of them were filled with the Holy Spirit and began to speak in other tongues as the Spirit enabled them. (*see* Acts 2:1–4)

Peter was one of those who "were filled with the Holy Spirit" that day. He provides an outstanding example of the empowerment that comes when one is filled with the Spirit of God. On the night before Jesus' crucifixion, Peter had denied the Lord three times; out of fear, he had refused to acknowledge even knowing Jesus. Once filled with the power of the Holy Spirit, however, the formerly fearful Peter preached publicly and boldly about the risen Lord to a vast crowd in Jerusalem, the very city in which Jesus had been crucified only weeks before! Peter's bold address to the crowd must have been inspiring because about three thousand people were baptized as a result of it (*see* Acts 2:41). An inarticulate fisherman like Peter could not have delivered his very powerful address to the crowd in Jerusalem had he not been given *power* from heaven.

For the Christian in recovery, only the Holy Spirit can give the power needed to carry out God's will for us in our daily lives. The aging Paul wrote to his beloved young friend, Timothy: "For God did not give us a spirit of timidity, but a spirit of power, of love and of self-discipline" (2 Tim. 1:7).

Paul's words apply equally to us today; the Spirit of God that resides in us is a spirit of *power,* and is the *source* of the power called for in Step Eleven.

As we seek to carry out God's will for our lives, we are promised the aid of the Holy Spirit. This does not mean, however, that God will do everything for us; each of us has his or her own part to play in the carrying out of God's will. Pastor Juan Carlos Ortiz offers a useful analogy to show how God works with us in a *combined* effort to facilitate the carrying out of his will. Consider the power brakes on a car. For power brakes to work, the driver need only press gently on the brake pedal to activate the hydraulic system. The fluids in the hydraulic system greatly multiply the gentle force used by the driver so as to bring the car to a stop. In the same way, the Holy Spirit *empowers* our efforts so that God's will can be done in our lives.[8]

God gave Peter the power to stand before a vast throng in Jerusalem and deliver an impassioned address, yet Peter had to muster the courage to overcome his inevitable fear and stand before the crowd. More than courage, great *faith* was required of this uneducated fisherman to enable him to do something he had never done before. Peter was speaking from personal experience when, many years after his impassioned address in Jerusalem, he wrote:

> His divine power has given us everything we need for life and godliness through our knowledge of him who called us by his own glory and goodness. (2 Pet. 1:3)

CHAPTER XIX

Step Twelve: The Program in a Nutshell

STEP TWELVE: *Having had a spiritual awakening as the result of these steps, we tried to carry this message to alcoholics, and to practice these principles in all our affairs.*

Addiction—whether chemical, behavioral, or relational—is first and foremost a *spiritual* disease. It is an attempt to escape the "pain, brokenness, and human limitation" of our existence in this fallen world.[1] Pain, brokenness, and human limitation are spiritual problems that emanate from the atrophy of the soul that characterizes human beings who have been cut off from the life-giving sustenance of the Creator.

Chemical dependency and other forms of addiction frequently result from maladaptive attempts to find the solace that comes only from a spiritual relationship with the God who is there. Addiction is often the unfortunate result of innumerable misguided attempts to fill the emptiness of our thirsty souls with chemicals or inappropriate behaviors.

Addiction is a spiritual disease because it offers a counterfeit substitute for the soul-healing that can come only from a personal relationship with Jesus Christ. In the words of St. Augustine, "Thou hast made us for Thyself, and the heart of man is restless until it finds its rest in Thee."[2]

A SPIRITUAL AWAKENING

Addiction is spiritual death; recovery is spiritual rebirth—an awakening and resurrection from the stale, cold death of addiction. God has called us "out of darkness into his wonderful light" (1 Pet. 2:9). Recovery is such a metamorphosis, a transition from darkness to light: "For you were once darkness, but now you are light in the Lord. Live as children of light" (Eph. 5:8). Like recovery, the transition from darkness to light is a spiritual awakening; thus, Paul writes, "Wake up, O sleeper, rise from the dead, and Christ will shine on you" (Eph. 5:14).

The spiritual awakening that results from the Twelve Steps varies in manner from person to person. Occasionally, it may occur in a moment of explosive spiritual insight or instantaneous awareness of one's aberrant, addictive behavior and the need for a major revision in one's manner of living. More commonly, however, spiritual awakening occurs gradually, as the pain and chaos of our addictive lifestyles force us to reevaluate our maladaptive manner of living. Regardless of how it occurs, however, it is important to remember that a spiritual awakening, like recovery itself, is an ongoing process—not a onetime event.

Spirituality

The discussion of a spiritual awakening necessitates an understanding of the concept of *spirituality.* Alcoholics

Anonymous and other Twelve-Step programs are invariably described as *spiritual* programs. Rarely, however, is one given the exact meaning of the term *spiritual* as used in the context of the Twelve Steps.

Spirituality can be described as "living in full awareness of the presence of God." It is an ongoing sense of *connectedness* with him, a continual awareness of living all of life in his presence. Moreover, spirituality is an ongoing process of surrender, of continually turning our will and our lives over to God. At the same time, spirituality is evidenced by manifestations of the "fruit of the Spirit" (*see* Gal. 5:22). Finally, to reduce it to its simplest terms, spirituality is walking as Christ walked (*see* 1 John 2:6).

This understanding of spirituality views both the Twelve Steps and the "way" that is called Christianity as identical paths through life. Recovering Christians who are active in Twelve-Step circles, then, need not compartmentalize their lives into two distinct and mutually exclusive parts; for Christians in recovery, the Twelve Steps and Christianity are the *same program.*

Practical Matters

In a practical sense, how may we know if we have experienced a spiritual awakening? How can we be sure we are practicing spiritual principles? One very good way of assessing our spirituality is to look for manifestations of the "fruit of the Spirit" in our daily lives: "love, joy, peace, patience, kindness, goodness, faithfulness, gentleness and self-control" (Gal. 5:22–23a). These behaviors are, of course, quite different from those associated with active addiction. Manifestations of any or all of these fruits of the Spirit are further evidence that one has had a spiritual awakening and is living a life characterized by spiritual principles.

Another means of assessing spirituality is to look at who is in charge of one's life. In this sense, spirituality means that the omnipotent, egocentric human nature inherent at birth has been subjugated to the Lordship of Jesus Christ; his majesty the baby has been dethroned and the King of kings is on the throne in our lives. Therefore, in this sense, spirituality is the daily, ongoing submission to the Lordship of Jesus Christ.

TO PRACTICE THESE PRINCIPLES

The principles that we are to practice are, of course, the Twelve Steps. As this book has intended to show, these are *biblical* principles, ones that characterize the lifestyle of genuine Christianity. We are "to practice these principles in all our affairs." The Twelve Steps are not designed to aid us in achieving abstinence from addictive substances and compulsive behaviors only; surely, if they did nothing more than that, their value would be immeasurable. However, the principles encompassed in these steps are amenable to far greater application than the achievement of abstinence only.

The Twelve Steps are principles of sane, healthy, abundant living and are applicable to every aspect of our lives. They inform every transaction of our relationships with God, others, and self. The principles embodied in these steps characterize the life of true spirituality: recognition of human need and limitation (Step One), faith in a Power greater than ourselves (Step Two), subjugation of self-will to Divine Will (Steps Three, Six, and Seven), self-examination or personal inventory (Steps Four and Ten), confession of sin (Step Five), healing and restoration of relationships with our fellow human beings (Steps Eight and Nine), prayer and meditation (Step Eleven), and social contribution (Step Twelve).

In the teaching of the Holy Bible itself, we are encouraged to practice these principles in all our affairs. The Apostle James wrote:

> Do not merely listen to the word, and so deceive yourselves. Do what it says. Anyone who listens to the word but does not do what it says is like a man who looks at his face in a mirror and, after looking at himself, goes away and immediately forgets what he looks like. But the man who looks intently into the perfect law that gives freedom, and continues to do this, not forgetting what he has heard, but doing it—he will be blessed in what he does. (James 1:22–25)

"The perfect law that gives freedom" is the law of love as summarized by Christ in the two great commandments. Love for God and love for neighbor and self is interwoven throughout the Twelve Steps. That's what makes it all work!

Failure to practice these spiritual principles in all our affairs is an invitation to disaster. If we fail to work the program, we are like a man or woman who looks into the mirror, sees the dirt on his or her face, and does nothing about it. If we wish to remain in recovery, we dare not walk away from the mirror and forget what we looked like when we were in the throes of active addiction.

The Apostle Paul wrote to the Christians in Rome: "offer your bodies as living sacrifices, holy and pleasing to God—this is your spiritual act of worship" (Rom. 12:1). There is no demand that is more characteristically Christian than this one.[3] The offering of our bodies as living sacrifices is what Paul calls our "spiritual act of worship." As William Barclay states, "True worship is the offering to God of one's body, and all that one does with it . . . A (person) may say, 'I am going to church to worship God,' but he should also be able to say, 'I am going to the factory, the shop, the office, the school, the garage . . . the garden, to worship God.' "[4] When Christians in recovery practice the principles of the Twelve Steps "in all our affairs," we are engaging in true worship. Worship, then, becomes a daily, ongoing process that is woven into the fabric of our lives—not a lifeless, irrelevant formality performed in a building of bricks and mortar on Sunday mornings! By presenting ourselves as living sacrifices to him, we are practicing spiritual principles in all our affairs.

Real Christianity or true spirituality is vastly different from the way of the secular society that surrounds us. To the world around us, "the message of the cross is foolishness" (1 Cor. 1:18). True spiritual living will seem strange and odd to those whose desires are dominated by the hedonism and rampant materialism of our society.

As Christians in recovery, we must follow a far different path than the deeply trodden and worn-out path of secular society. Furthermore, we must aspire to a deeper spirituality than that of those who pursue a watered-down form of "Christianity," calling Jesus "Lord" but not doing the things he says (*see* Luke 6:46). For us, these principles may not be practiced on a part-time or halfhearted basis; for those of us in recovery from addiction, these principles are matters of life or death!

TO CARRY THIS MESSAGE

Not only must we practice these principles in all our affairs, but we must carry the message to others; thus, the "twelfth-step call" is an important part of recovery. The twelfth-step call occurs when someone in recovery talks to or visits another person still trapped in active addiction. The twelfth-step recoverer carries the message of recovery by sharing his or her strength, hope, and experience with the practicing addict. It is hoped that the addict, upon seeing and hearing of the changes in the twelfth-step recoverer's life, will desire to embark on a program of recovery as well.

The primary beneficiary of the twelfth-step call, however, is not the person still trapped in addiction, but rather the one making the call. Bill Wilson, the founder of Alcoholics Anonymous, discovered that the only way he could stay sober was to talk to other alcoholics. Today, his example is followed countless times daily.

Step Twelve is an application of the paradoxical principle that to keep what we have, we must give it away. This is the meaning of Jesus' enigmatic statement, "whoever loses his life for me will find it" (Matt. 16:25). Twelfth-step work is a manifestation of spirituality. Whenever we operate in the spiritual realm, the rules change: to keep it, give it away; to find it, lose it; to increase, then first decrease; to be great, become a servant; to be first, then be last! The kingdom of God, the realm of true spirituality, is, indeed, a "Kingdom of paradox."[5]

The rules of the spiritual realm become more understandable, however, when we remember that the essential ingredient in spirituality is love—love emanating from the Father, through the Son, and manifested in us by the work of the Holy Spirit. For love to increase, it must be shared. Love for God and mankind is the heart of Christian living and the basis for true spirituality. In the renowned words of the Apostle Paul:

> If I speak in the tongues of men and of angels, but have not love, I am only a resounding gong or a clanging cymbal. If I have the gift of prophecy and can fathom all mysteries and all knowledge, and if I have a faith that can move mountains, but have not love, I am nothing. If I give all I possess to the

> poor and surrender my body to the flames, but have not love, I gain nothing. Love is patient, love is kind. It does not envy, it does not boast, it is not proud. It is not rude, it is not self-seeking, it is not easily angered, it keeps no record of wrongs. Love does not delight in evil but rejoices with the truth. It always protects, always trusts, always hopes, always perseveres. Love never fails . . . And now these three remain: faith, hope and love. But the greatest of these is love. (1 Cor. 13:1–8a, 13)

Love increases in direct proportion to the amount given away. Therefore, Paul's immortal words apply as equally to the person in A.A. making a twelfth-step call as to the evangelical Christian sharing the Good News about Jesus Christ.

We have seen that, for Christians in recovery, the twelve steps and the Christian walk are identical paths—not two distinct aspects of living to be compartmentalized into separate arenas, but a common way of life. When we make a twelfth-step call, we may share not only the program of recovery as outlined in the Twelve Steps, but also the Good News of the love of God for all people, as manifested in the person of Jesus Christ. Depending on the nature of the situation, the Twelve Steps may be used as a bridge to the Gospel or the Gospel may be used as a bridge to the Twelve Steps. For Christians in recovery, the Gospel and the Twelve Steps are inseparable; they intertwine with one another to form the cord that connects us to our Higher Power, Jesus Christ.

As Christians in recovery, we carry *one* message to those still trapped in addiction. Whether conveyed in the language of the Twelve Steps as revealed in *The Big Book* or in the language of the Gospel as revealed in the Holy Bible, we carry the message of healing and salvation through Jesus Christ. We have a unique opportunity in obeying the command of our Lord to "go and make disciples of all nations"

(Matt. 28:19). Because of our common background of addiction, we may share our experience, strength, and hope—and the Good News about Jesus Christ!

> Praise be to the God and Father of our Lord Jesus Christ, the Father of compassion and the God of all comfort, who comforts us in all our troubles, so that we can comfort those in any trouble with the comfort we ourselves have received from God. (2 Cor. 1:3–4)

Endnotes

INTRODUCTION

1. John Keller, *Ministering to Alcoholics* (Minneapolis: Augsburg Publishing House, 1991), 37.

2. John Keller, *Let Go, Let God* (Minneapolis: Augsburg Publishing House, 1985), 13–17.

3. *Alcoholics Anonymous,* 3d ed. (New York: A.A. World Services, 1976), xxii.

4. Keller, *Let Go, Let God,* 56–57.

CHAPTER I: THE JOURNEY BEGINS

1. Keller, *Let Go, Let God,* 32.

2. Ibid., 33.

3. Ibid., 35.

4. Ibid., 36.

5. Ibid., 37.

6. Stephen Van Cleave, Walter Byrd, and Kathy Revell, *Counseling for Substance Abuse and Addiction,* Resources for Christian Counseling, ed. Gary Collins, vol. 12 (Waco, TX: Word Books, 1987), 19–26.

7. Sandra D. Wilson, *Counseling Adult Children of Alcoholics,* Resources for Christian Counseling, ed. Gary Collins, vol. 21 (Dallas: Word Publishing, 1989), 4.

CHAPTER II: DESCENT INTO POWERLESSNESS

1. Charles Colson, *Loving God* (Grand Rapids: Zondervan Publishing House, 1983), 24–25.

CHAPTER V: FAITH

1. *Alcoholics Anonymous,* 63.
2. Billy Graham, *Peace with God* (Waco, TX: Word Books, 1984), 132–34.
3. Ibid., 134.

CHAPTER VI: GOD AS WE UNDERSTAND HIM

1. Wilson, *Counseling Adult Children,* 95–100.
2. Ibid., 100–102.

CHAPTER VII: GETTING INTO THE WHEELBARROW

1. *Alcoholics Anonymous,* 63.
2. Keller, *Let Go, Let God,* 35.
3. Ibid., 44.
4. Ibid., 53.
5. Ibid., 53.
6. Ibid., 45.
7. William Barclay, *The Letter to the Romans,* The Daily Study Bible (Philadelphia: The Westminster Press, 1975), 157.

CHAPTER VIII: THE RICH YOUNG MAN

1. William Blake, "The Garden of Love," in *Selected Poetry and Prose of William Blake,* ed. Nothrop Frye (New York: The Modern Library, Random House, 1953), 45.
2. David Seamands, *Healing Grace* (Wheaton, IL: Victor Books, 1988), 111–13.
3. Francis A. Schaeffer, *How Should We Then Live?* (Old Tappan, NJ: Fleming H. Revell Co., 1976).
4. George MacDonald, *365 Readings,* edited and with a preface by C.S. Lewis (New York: Collier Books, Macmillan Publishing Co., 1947), 27.

CHAPTER IX: LET THE SON SHINE IN

1. Keller, *Let Go, Let God,* 13ff.
2. Ibid., 58.
3. Ibid., 86.
4. Ibid., 59.

CHAPTER X: LIABILITIES: PRIDE, GREED, AND LUST

1. *Step 4: Guide to Fourth Step Inventory* (Center City, MN: Hazelden Foundation, 1973). While the Seven Cardinal Sins provide a broad and useful framework for evaluating liabilities, a more narrow focus is also beneficial. Hazelden's pamphlet provides a detailed look at numerous areas that should be explored as part of the fourth step inventory. Though targeted primarily for alcoholics, this pamphlet is useful for all Twelve-Steppers taking the fourth step. The pamphlet is available from Hazelden Educational Materials, Box 176, Center City, MN 55012.
2. Ibid., 7.
3. MacDonald, *365 Readings,* 31.
4. Ibid., 10.

5. Ibid., 32.
6. *Step 4: Guide,* 7.

CHAPTER XI: LIABILITIES: ENVY, ANGER, GLUTTONY, AND SLOTH

1. *Step 4: Guide,* 4.
2. Ibid., 8.

CHAPTER XII: ASSETS: A NEW CREATION

1. Robert S. McGee, *The Search for Significance,* 2d ed. (Houston: Rapha Publishing, 1990), 53.
2. Barclay, *Romans,* 159.
3. Ibid., 159.
4. Ibid., 159.
5. Ibid., 160.
6. Ibid., 160–61.
7. MacDonald, *365 Readings,* 8–9.

CHAPTER XIII: CONFESSION

1. Robert Johnstone, *A Commentary on James* (Carlisle, PA: Banner of Truth Trust, 1871), 41.
2. William Barclay, *The Letters of John and Jude,* The Daily Study Bible (Philadelphia: The Westminster Press, 1958), 39.
3. Ibid., 39.
4. Ibid., 39.
5. J. Vernon McGee, *Psalms,* vol. 2 (Pasadena: Through the Bible Books, 1977), 57.
6. Barclay, *John and Jude,* 39.
7. Ibid., 40.
8. William Barclay, *The Letters of James and Peter,* The Daily Study Bible (Philadelphia: The Westminster Press, 1958), 155.

9. Ibid., 154.
10. Edward C. Sellner, *Step 5: A Guide to Reconciliation* (Center City, MN: Hazelden Foundation, 1981), 10.
11. Ibid., 8.
12. Keller, *Let Go, Let God,* 87.

CHAPTER XIV: ENTIRELY READY, HUMBLY ASKED

1. James Brandon, *Steps 6 & 7: The Forgotten Steps* (Center City, MN: Hazelden Foundation, 1981), 12.
2. Ibid., 9.
3. Ibid., 9.
4. Ibid., 7.
5. MacDonald, *365 Readings,* 68.
6. McGee, *Psalms,* 58.

CHAPTER XV: MAKING AMENDS

1. Pat M., *Step 8: Restoring Relationships* (Center City, MN: Hazelden Foundation, 1982), 8.
2. Pat M., *Step 9: Making Amends* (Center City, MN: Hazelden Foundation, 1982), 4.
3. William Barclay, *The Gospel of Matthew,* vol. 1, The Daily Study Bible (Philadelphia: The Westminster Press, 1956), 140–41.
4. Pat M., *Step 9: Making Amends,* 8.
5. MacDonald, *365 Readings,* 51.
6. "The Prayer of St. Francis," in Pat M., *Step 9,* 12.

CHAPTER XVI: A DAILY STRUGGLE

1. Mel B., *Step 10: A Good Tenth Step* (Center City, MN: Hazelden Foundation, 1982), 6.
2. Barclay, *The Gospel of Matthew,* 135–36.

3. Ibid., 142.
4. Mel B., *Step 10,* 13.
5. Ibid., 13–14.

CHAPTER XVII: PRAYER AND MEDITATION

1. C.S. Lewis, *The Joyful Christian* (New York: Collier Books, Macmillan Publishing Co., 1977), 89.
2. MacDonald, *365 Readings,* 101.
3. Patrick M. Morley, *I Surrender* (Brentwood, TN: Wolgemuth & Hyatt, Publishers, 1990), 149.
4. Ibid., 152.
5. Ibid., 167.
6. Ibid., 167.
7. MacDonald, *365 Readings,* 27.

CHAPTER XVIII: KNOWLEDGE OF HIS WILL

1. Morley, *I Surrender,* 131.
2. Ibid., 132.
3. Ibid., 133.
4. D. Martin Lloyd-Jones, *Studies in the Sermon on the Mount,* vol. 2 (Grand Rapids: Wm. B. Eerdmans Publishing Co., 1960), 204.
5. Ibid., 204.
6. MacDonald, *365 Readings,* 46–47.
7. Ibid., 46.
8. Gordon Dalbey, *Healing the Masculine Soul* (Dallas: Word Publishing, 1988), 95.

CHAPTER XIX: STEP 12: THE PROGRAM IN A NUTSHELL

1. Keller, *Let Go, Let God,* 13ff.

2. St. Augustine, *Confessions,* quoted in W. Neil, ed., *Concise Dictionary of Religious Quotations* (Grand Rapids: Wm. B. Eerdmans, 1974), 60.

3. Barclay, *Romans,* 156.

4. Ibid., 157.

5. Colson, *Loving God,* 25.